Reid Jepson's Devotional Dictionary

Volume I

Promise Publishing Co.
Orange CA 92665

Reid Jepson's Devotional Dictionary
Copyright 1993 by Promise Publishing Co.
Orange CA 92665

Edited by M.B. Steele

Printed in the United States of America

ALL RIGHTS RESERVED. No part of this publication may be reproduced, stored in a retrieval system or transmitted in any form or by any means, electronic, mechanical, photo-copying or otherwise without the prior, written consent of the publisher.

Scripture is from The Holy Bible, King James Version.
Copyright 1967 by Oxford University, Inc., publisher.

Library of Congress Cataloging-in-Publication Data

Jepson, Reid
        Reid Jepson's Devotional Dictionary

ISBN 0-939497-31-X

Foreword

A unique approach in devotional books, "Reid Jepson's Devotional Dictionary" focuses on the important words and concepts in the Word of God.

Originally given to an international radio audience, these brief messages assist you in knowing God better and wanting to serve Him with greater devotion. New believers as well as seasoned saints will find these truths stimulating and encouraging in these difficult days.

Further, Reid presents the basis for many devotional talks and messages. An individual or a group can be led in a time of worship and praise by using the material you will find in this inspirational book.

Warren Wiersbe, Author
Formerly Moody Church, Pastor
Back to the Bible, Speaker

Others Speak

Reid Jepson has a heart of compassion for God and His work worldwide. For many years, Reid has "felt" missions, "talked" missions, "prayed" missions and "ministered" missions ... at home and around the world. Through many years of faithful service to the Lord of the harvest, Reid has written and aired these messages over radio stations in the United States as well as over Far East Broadcasting stations in Asia and TransWorld Radio stations in Europe.

"Reid Jepson's Devotional Dictionary" is filled with short and to-the-point talks based on the Word of God. Interesting anecdotes are liberally sprinkled throughout. You will find this unique book both inspirational and devotional for your quiet times with the Lord. I commend it to you wholeheartedly.

> Robert Bowman, Pres. Em.
> Far East Broadcasting

Reid Jepson has put together a very unique book of devotions which include definitions, explanations, and doctrines of the Bible. This is good for preachers, believers and non-believers. What a reservoir of biblical truth to be so compact in one volume!

> T. W. Wilson
> Associate to Billy Graham

Many of us look for new ways to approach God's holy Word - to gain wisdom, insight, guidance and instruction. Longtime friend Reid Jepson has uniquely helped us to apply "definitions" devotionally to key scriptural, biblical terms. My personal thanks go to Reid for this valid and valuable contribution.

> Ted W. Engstrom, Pres. Em.
> World Vision

Acknowledgments

The Bible-based commentaries included in this book were developed for broadcasts for a number of foreign and domestic radio stations. Responses like the following have encouraged us to publish the content of those programs:

While travelling, I heard your message. I would like to have a copy of the one on loneliness.   Ohio

I appreciate your good lessons. I wish I were able to assist you.
        Washington

I was simply thrilled as I heard your program. I copied down as much as I could.

We gain much knowledge from your short and enlightening radio program.   Philippines

A number of writers over a period of four decades have contributed to these articles. Especially helpful was a long time friend and colleague, David Enlow, editor and author.

Some lines have been adapted from honored publications such as Our Daily Bread, books by Moody Press and various Christian magazines. We are grateful for all sources whether specifically identified or not. Some material has been so widely used it is difficult to determine its actual origin.

Our desire is that readers will be influenced toward salvation in Christ, consecration for holy living and Christian service at home and abroad.

Introduction

Anyone who has been paying attention has noticed that there are a great many opinions about Scripture, religion and God, and they are widely divergent. Whenever any two people come together to take a look at God's Word, they need to find the things on which they can agree and begin their search into God's riches from that point.

In order to be sure that the reader and I are in tune on at least the basic teaching of Scripture, I have presented a few pages of definitions which seem to me to be essential in our approach to a devotional look at the Bible. These few pages are designed to bring us to a basic understanding and agreement on the terms and concepts needed to proceed into the rest of our inspirational journey. Words like "Christian" and "God" need to bring to your mind (and mine) a mental picture consistent with the teaching of the Bible.

In order to try to achieve this lofty goal, we'll first consider a few of the basic words of Scripture and the scriptural meaning for them. The pages are not dated so you can begin any day of the year.

The balance of the words chosen for inclusion in this book have been taken at random from the 773,746 words used in the King James Version of the Holy Bible.

Let us take aim at surefooted passage among the words of the Bible.

Reid Jepson

ADAM

Defined as "the first man; the father of the human race", this name is used in the New Testament to symbolize the human tendency to sin. All of us have descended from Adam and Eve. No matter what route we trace our ancestry, part of us has been inherited from the first parents. Since Adam was "made a living soul", we, too, have a soul handed down to us from him.

This name means "of the ground" since God formed him from the dust and Eve, the woman, was formed from his rib. Together they began the chain of humanity which reaches to the billions of people on earth today. With all our differences, we are the same.

When God made Adam, He made him in His own image. He wanted Adam (and us) to be like Him. This isn't true of animals and the rest of the creation that God made - they were not made in God's image. Only man is said to be "like God", and even though Adam sinned, he retained the basic form of God and passed that along to each of us. Man is God's masterpiece - the crowning work of creation.

Jesus is contrasted as "the second Adam", a heavenly Adam who is "the Lord". Like Adam, He is head of a family, but His family is a spiritual one and each member of His family possesses spiritual life. "In Adam all die" because "the wages of sin is death". Just as we received the image of God from Adam, so we also received a sinful nature from him. However, since Christ was raised from the dead, we receive life when we receive Jesus. In Christ "all shall be made alive" because "in Him is life". He is "...the Life" (Jn. 14:6).

REMEMBER: You already have physical life, and you can receive spiritual life from Christ today. Call on His name!

ZEAL

This old-fashioned word is often used in the Bible and, even though we don't use it much ourselves these days, it captures the essence of enthusiasm in its purest form. Although it has many good connotations, zeal can also lead the zealot into trouble by going too far, ignoring all other considerations. There are examples of both found in the Bible.

Jehu and David were said to "have zeal for the Lord" and Isaiah speaks of God being "clad with zeal as with a cloak". Paul commended the church at Corinth because they had zeal and because of their zeal, they were "a good example to others".

But Paul also said of himself that he had been zealous in persecuting the church - he had been zealous, but wrong. Paul also said that the Jews have a "zeal for God, but not according to knowledge". Herein is the word of caution - zeal without knowledge (and good judgment) can be a harmful thing. In our zeal, it is possible that we "thrust our calloused hand among the heartstrings of a friend" doing more harm than good even when our intentions were of the highest order. There is surely nothing wrong with enthusiasm and vitality. However, if they are unleashed without being tempered with knowledge and good judgment, awareness of others and compassion, they do more harm than good.

There is no virtue in apathy. Nothing much worthwhile is accomplished without enthusiasm, so let's put our hands to work for God with a great deal of zeal while still keeping our wits about us. We can avoid the pitfalls of extremism even while working enthusiastically for good and for God.

REMEMBER: Go from A to Z - Apathy to Zeal - in the service of Jesus Christ.

GOD

God has been described as everything from "the eternal good" to "a consuming fire". There seems to be no universal definition of God. He is clearly someone supernatural and a person to be be worshipped, but there the similarity of descriptions ends. Even the Bible does not describe God, nor argue for His existence - it assumes that God is and proceeds to tell what He has done and what He cares to communicate to us. We must draw our conclusions of who He is from that.

- Genesis starts by telling us that He created the world and everything in it, so we conclude that He is the Creator.

- Friendship with Adam and Eve is described, so we draw from that the implication that He wants to be friends with us.

- He condemned their sin and it separated them from fellowship with God. We must conclude that His reaction to our sin is the same and that a sacrifice is required to restore our relationship just as was required of Abel.

- Cain's offering was rejected, and it shows that the sacrifice must be the one God asked for - a lamb, a spotless lamb.

- Noah portrays for us that God will punish sin while, at the same time, providing a way out for those who love Him and obey Him whatever the cost.

- Abraham acted out a father's sacrifice of his son and, in time, God gave His Son, Jesus, as a sacrifice for sin and called Him, "The Lamb of God who takes away the sin of the world." Can you see God's loving heart? It's pictured on the pages of Scripture for all to see.

REMEMBER: Get your definition of God from the Bible, not from your imagination.

JEHOVAH

One way of getting to know God is by way of His names. He has lots of names, one of which is Jehovah. This Old Testament name conveys to us the fact that He has always been and always will be in existence. This name appears more than 6,000 times in the Old Testament which tells us the importance of this name for God. So sacred was this name for God to people in those days that they refused to utter it aloud. According to tradition, the name Jehovah was pronounced only once a year by the High Priest on the Day of Atonement.

When God appeared to Moses in the burning bush to commission him to lead the Children of Israel, He said, "I AM THAT I AM." God is who He is - unlike anyone else, not to be compared with anyone. His life is not derived from anyone; He just IS, and He always WAS. How different from our lives which are derived from our parents and had a very specific beginning!

In talking to Job, God asked Job what he thought God might want to do that He could not do. It is clear that Job had no answer for that one–nor do we! God can do whatever He chooses and no one can stop Him or force Him to change His actions, yet God invites us to "reason together" with Him and Abraham (among others) got God to change His mind by his petitions. Also, a prophet, though a mere man, asked God to withhold the rain, and God changed the weather patterns that He Himself had made. God invites us to come to Him, asking whatever we want to ask, and we know that He will hear us and answer according to His will. Let's not be in want for lack of asking God for the things we need!

REMEMBER: God's power is beyond us, but He loves us so much, He gives us what we ask for.

JEHOVAH SHALOM

This name of God means "God is our peace". Gideon built an altar which he called by this name for God. Gideon was a timid man who met the Angel of the Lord face to face, and feared for his life because of it. He and all the Israelites were already afraid because of their enemies, but they were also afraid of God because they had not been pleasing Him as they knew they should. They had seen God punish His people before by giving their enemies power to conquer them in battle. It looked like God was going to do it again. Nevertheless, when Gideon met the Angel of the Lord, he found peace so he called the altar which he built, "God is our peace".

When we have God with us, we have peace.

As a small child, I got lost on a family outing. We had gone to a small state park and being an adventurous child, I ran ahead on the path when suddenly I realized that I was alone. I began to cry. Then, along came my Uncle Morris to sweep me up in his strong arms. Safe in his familiar grip, the sight of my parents soon calmed my fears and returned peace and calm to my troubled, little boy heart. As grown-ups, we are sometimes afraid - and with good reason! Still, the presence of Jehovah-Shalom is enough to bring us peace in spite of the problems. He comforts us no matter what our circumstances.

The Roman world into which Jesus was born was full of fear - Romans were ruthless conquerors - so the angels said, "A Savior is born! Glory to God in the highest and on earth, peace ...." This was Jehovah-Shalom who had come to earth to make peace **with** God, to give peace **from** God and to enable us to experience the peace **of** God in our hearts.

REMEMBER: You can come to our loving God today and find peace for your fearful heart.

CHRIST

Jesus said that He is God, "I and my Father are One." Still, the mission of Jesus Christ on earth was unique; He came as the One anointed to carry out God's plan which had been in place before the world began. His names, "the Christ" and "the Messiah", mean "anointed" - one is Greek, the other Hebrew.

In the Old Testament, many of God's servants were anointed to carry out the work that God had assigned to them. Some were kings, some were prophets, some were priests. King David was called "God's anointed" by Samuel. The Children of Israel were called "the Lord's anointed" people. Jesus, the Messiah, is God's perfect king, His perfect prophet, and His perfect priest. Jesus is the King of kings.

Amid the confusion and differences of opinion concerning Jesus while He lived in Galilee, Jesus went to a synagogue in Nazareth on one special Sabbath day. As was the custom, He stood to read from the Torah, and He read from Isaiah concerning the One who was to come from God as the Anointed One.

Jesus broke off His reading mid-sentence. In the puzzled silence of the moment, Jesus said, "Today this has been fulfilled in your midst" - He laid claim to the title, "The Anointed One". He left no doubt about it - we can believe it or not, but He clearly claimed to be God's Anointed One.

Jesus said, *"I am come that they might have life and have it more abundantly."* His assignment from the Father was to give His life so that we might be freed from the penalty of death - and more than that, He wants us to live happily and fully, enjoying all that God has made for us - the world and all that is in it.

REMEMBER: God called on His Son to carry out a special work - He died for us.

CHRISTIAN

When it was first used, this "tag" was enunciated with a sneer. Their enemies coined the name for those early followers of Christ. To the surprise of the multitudes, those who believed in Jesus welcomed the privilege of carrying His name. After all, just as Christ was anointed of God to fulfill His plan, just so Jesus' disciples were sent by Jesus to carry the Gospel to all the world. *"As the Father has sent Me, so send I you,"* Jesus said to them. It is an honor to serve Him and to bear His name.

King Agrippa used the name when Paul nearly persuaded him to believe, "Almost you persuade me to be a Christian." Paul had explained that Jesus died in Agrippa's place (and ours) to take away sin. We all must make a choice. Agrippa only came close. "Almost" is not enough. (Read the story in Acts 26.)

The disciples were called Christians the first time at Antioch where their behavior was so changed that they reminded everyone of Christ, Himself. To truly choose Christ means a real change from what we would have been without Him. The disciples were sent to do a special task just as Jesus Christ had been. Their challenge was to carry the Good News of salvation to the world, yet there are still millions who have not yet heard what Jesus did for them.

Have you come to believe in Christ as your Savior? Would you join in the worldwide task of taking His name and His gospel to the ends of the earth? We are to be witnesses to Him in Judea (Hometown, USA), Samaria (our part of the country), and to the ends of the earth - that's all inclusive. Every person who lives on this earth needs to know about Jesus and how can they hear if we don't tell them?

REMEMBER: Choosing Christ means that we change, and we accept His challenge to spread the gospel.

Reid Jepson's Devotional Dictionary

Now that we have the "ground rules" spelled out, we can begin our alphabetical approach to biblical inspiration. Nothing is so basic to communication as the words we use to express ourselves. Many of the people who have believed the Bible throughout the centuries of history have believed in "the plenary verbal inspiration of the Scriptures". That is, believers take the Bible to have been expressed in the exact words which God selected to communicate with us.

We're all aware that the Bible was originally written in the Hebrew language and the Greek language with only a small portion in Daniel in Aramaic. That presents to the reader of the English Bible a challenge which requires some study and understanding to ferret out the depth of meaning that has (in some cases) been covered with the dust of time and translation.

Not that we cannot accept our Bibles for what they say. We can! God laid it on the hearts of godly men (in most cases) to translate Scripture into English and other languages so that we can read it in our "mother tongue". His mighty hand has guarded and guided those who have undertaken to bring His word to us in our own language. When we take a close look at the words we find there, it brings blessing to our hearts. My hope is that this will be only the first volume of other such studies.

Embark with me now on a voyage into some of the beautiful coves and harbors of God's Word where we will find "buried treasure" to enrich our lives.

ALL

Here's a useful little word that can be an adjective, a pronoun, a noun or an adverb. One of the Bible verses where this word is most effective is Isaiah 53:6,

"ALL we like sheep have gone astray, we have turned every one to his own way, and the Lord has laid on Him the iniquity of us ALL."

This verse begins and ends with ALL - we enter as one of all the lost sheep and take our place among all those whose sins have been forgiven. Anyone can be included for *"all have sinned"* and Jesus paid the price for all our sins. But that's not all!

Paul tells us that all that God has is ours - what an inheritance! We're also promised that *"All things work together for good"* for God's children. Even so, most of us respond by giving Him only a part of our hearts and lives. How rare it was when a poor widow put ALL she had into the offering box in the temple. Jesus saw it and said that she had given more than everyone else - she gave all she had, all her living. She came closer than anyone else to giving back to Jesus what He had given for her - His ALL.

Everything we are and everything we have comes from God. It is reasonable for us to *"present our bodies a living sacrifice, holy acceptable to Him"*. How can we callously return only part of it to Him? *"Whatsoever your hand finds to do, do it with your might,"* Paul wrote. Christ is looking for a wholehearted response to His invitation to live our lives for Him. Like Paul, let us count everything a loss except what we do in service for our beloved Savior. Let's make our lives count for Jesus.

REMEMBER: One day, God will put all things "under Him" (Jesus) so that "God may be all in all."

APOSTLE

This name for the disciples means "a sent one". It refers to the challenge God gave us to "go into all the world and preach the gospel to everyone." Many Christians travel a lot. The Apostle Paul set the example. The longest he stayed in any one city after he accepted God's claim on his life was the two years that he stayed in Ephesus. The city served as a base of operations for the founding of many churches "throughout all Asia" in obedience to Christ who is the Supreme Apostle (see Heb. 3:1).

Paul and his co-workers worked together to spread the word of Jesus' life, death and resurrection. Even Paul's letters were written with the help of his fellow disciples. His journeys were made with a team of travelers and the churches were built with helpers of all kinds. He taught us that we all need each other and that we all serve different functions in the body of Christ. He was willing to reach out to diverse groups in a manner that appealed to each one individually. Paul changed his methods to fit the target audience. Only the "Word of truth" remained unchanged (read Matthew 10 to see the full meaning).

Today we see doctors and nurses using medicine to find entry for the Gospel. We see teachers reaching out to their students with the Truth while meeting the needs of their ignorance. We see counsellors dealing with family and personal problems in order to comfort the needy with God's message of love. This use of every means available to reach others with the Gospel is a pattern that Paul gave us as an example. He said, "I am all things to all people that by all means, I might win some." When we enter a person's life to meet a need they know they have, we can bring the Gospel to meet the needs of their hearts.

REMEMBER: Apostles are sent out by God with a message of life and hope.

ARMOR

We've all seen pictures of knights encased in the metal suits they called "armor". In their search for protection, it seems they have made it almost impossible to move at all! Despite the fact that it could not have been comfortable to wear the armor, it was a sign that they had made themselves available to fight and die (if need be) for a cause.

Christian's have armor, too, and it is designed for our protection in fighting the devil and his angels. It is spiritual armor and it enables us to stand against all odds. Our armor is truth, righteousness, faith, salvation, the gospel of peace and the sword of the Spirit (the Word of God—Rom. 6). We are commanded to stand - "having done all, to stand" - there is no armor for our backs that we could retreat.

The young David indicated his willingness to fight Goliath, the Philistine giant, so they tried to put metal armor on him. His small frame could not carry such weight. Instead, David put on "the armor of faith" and armed himself only with his shepherd's staff and a sling, picking up four stones on his way to battle. What would protect this boy so bravely going out to face a ten-foot giant of a man? His faith kept him safe:

"This day will the Lord deliver you into my hand; and all shall know that the Lord saveth not with sword and spear; for the battle is the Lord's" (I Sam. 17:46).

David had faced wild animals much stronger than himself, and God had allowed him to kill them. David knew that God could give the victory to whomsoever He chose and God's choice depended on the condition of the soldier's heart!

REMEMBER: "The battle is the Lord's". We can have victory by His power when we fight in His name.

ASSURANCE

The word "assurance" only appears in the King James Bible *six times*, but the words that appear with it are interesting.

• Isaiah says that assurance is the result of *righteousness* (Isa. 32:17). This seems to say that if we have no guilt to rattle us, we can face life calmly and confidently.

• Hebrews speaks of "the full assurance of *faith*" and, once again, we see that assurance is vitally linked with our relationship to God. After all, righteousness is only available to us when we place our faith in Jesus Christ, otherwise we are condemned - "for all have sinned". When we believe "to the saving of our souls", we no longer have need to fear the coming judgment of sin.

• Death loses its dread for us since we know that we will spend eternity with Jesus. Fear of others diminishes as well since pleasing God is now our goal instead of trying to please people. He is well pleased with a life of faith. The Bible teaches that He rewards those who live by faith, and He gives us *peace*.

• Another phrase we find is "the full assurance of *understanding*". One of life's tragedies is that some who believe have not gone on to gain understanding of the riches in Christ.

• One of these "riches" is "the full assurance of *hope*" spoken of in Hebrews. Our past sin and failure is gone so we have assurance. We know whose we are and what He gives us so the present is no longer fearful for us.

• We have hope for the future which gives us the *confidence* that our lives will have a good outcome no matter what trials we endure in the meantime.

REMEMBER: Assurance makes optimists out of us all.

BALM

Though we seldom use this wonderful word, it was well known in the ancient world.

The men who purchased Joseph from his brothers were taking spices and balm to Egypt (Gen. 37). Years later, when his father sent those same brothers to Egypt to buy food, he sent balm and spices as gifts to please the man (Joseph) who controlled the supply. The present was designed to curry his favor, but instead, it must have reminded Joseph of his journey to Egypt among the spices of the traders who owned him then. Even with the passing years, Joseph remembered his brothers and the way they "sold him out" because of their jealousy. Nevertheless, Joseph had forgiven his brothers and had seen the hand of God in everything that had happened to him. The "Balm of Gilead" (Jer. 46:11) had soothed and healed the soul of Joseph.

Medicines were used for healing even in those days, but just as today, there are those wounds and diseases which cannot be healed by any balm known to men. How helpless the physician whose prescriptions are of no effect.

There is a "Balm in Gilead", however, whose healing is beyond anything known to man - then or now. Jesus is that balm and His healing is for the body - and for the soul. While He lived in Galilee, He "healed all that came to Him" - "He healed them all" (Matt. 8:17).

In the same way, Jesus heals the hearts and souls of all that come to Him today. He often heals our sicknesses, but more importantly He provides that healing that no one else can give - a cure for sin.

REMEMBER: Cover yourself with His truth. Apply it as salve for the soul.

BAPTIZE

Does baptism seem to you to be optional for those who believe? This Greek word has been taken into our language without an English meaning, so we must find understanding of it in the way it was used by the Greeks.

- Classically, it was used of a ship that sank and was never again floated to the surface.

- It is used of a mythical bird, shot with an arrow, whose blood saturated the clouds and dyed them red.

These illustrations indicate that the former condition of the thing that was "baptized" was changed forever by the saturation it experienced. The basic condition of the object never returns to what was once "normal".

This gives us insight into what Paul meant when he said that when we're baptized into Jesus Christ, we now walk in "newness of life" (Rom. 6:4). We aren't ever the same again. Our old, dried up selves are saturated with the life which only Christ can give. Our skeptical, cynical selves are filled with hope, faith, assurance and love.

Our once colorless existence is now dyed with the brilliance of His life. Jesus has saturated our thoughts, our motives, our actions until they are scarcely recognizable as coming from us. Paul said, "I live, yet not I, but Christ lives in me." He was so saturated with Christ that his life was no longer his own - it was Christ's life in Paul's body. God's will was carried out by Paul's hands and feet and by his mouth as he spoke the truth of God to all who would hear. Paul was "dyed" by his relationship to Christ.

REMEMBER: Christ wants to live in you. Have you been "baptized into Christ"?

BELIEVE

Everyone believes in something, but WHAT we believe in is of vital importance.

- We can place our faith in a doctor, only to find that there is a limit to what he can do to help us.

- We can place our faith in a preacher, only to find that he, too, is able to fail and fall.

- We can trust a business partner, and find he has taken all that we owned.

But when we believe in Jesus, we find that there is no disappointment in Him. No, we don't always understand what He is doing in our lives, and we still suffer hardship in life; however, in Christ, we find these things are for our profit; not designed to hurt us, but to help us.

Believing in Christ is the conviction that what He said is true and we can rely on His Word. Believing makes us give up our own ideas and live in the light of what Jesus said. We take His word for what has been, what now is and what is to come. We yield ourselves to His work in our lives - no matter what others say or do ... no matter how things seem to be ... no matter how we feel at a given moment.

Believing also drives us to find out what Jesus had to say about the things we're facing in our lives today. How can we believe Him if we aren't sure what He said? We're driven to **ask** His guidance, to **seek** our answers among His teachings, to **knock** at the door of His wisdom. He only tells us what is true for *"God cannot lie"*.

REMEMBER: Jesus said, "I am ... the truth...." We can safely believe in Him.

BODY

Physical fitness is a passion for many people today. Eating "right" and exercising take up a great deal of energy, time and money, and yet the parameters change with each new discovery in this field.

"Cleanliness is next to godliness" the old timers used to say, placing being clean next to the top of their list of priorities. This concept is scriptural since the Bible teaches us that our bodies are the temple of the Holy Spirit and what we do in and to our bodies is important. We are instructed to keep our bodies clean (as in bathing) and clean as in doing what is right before God. "The body is for the Lord," we are told, and we are challenged to present our bodies as "a living sacrifice, holy, acceptable to God".

God, the Father, prepared the body in which Jesus was born. He came as a baby and his body grew to manhood, complete with scrapes and bumps, cuts and bruises. His body was like our bodies - completely human. He was tired and hungry, he slept and ate just as we live. "Yet [He was] without sin," the Bible says, for He was "God with us". That's the mystery - the thing we can't understand - He was completely human and truly God at the same time.

How amazing, then, that He allowed rough Roman soldiers to nail Him to a crude cross to die. His body hung in shame before a crowd of mockers. They gambled at His feet for His seamless cloak. He had no sin of His own for which He had to die, so He was in a position to die for our sins - and He did. "Who His own self bore our sins in His own body on the tree, that we, being dead to sins, should live unto righteousness; by whose stripes you were healed" (I Peter 2:24).

REMEMBER: "Present your bodies a living sacrifice ... to God, which is your reasonable service" (Rom. 12:1).

BOOK

When capitalized, "The Book" refers to the Holy Scriptures, the Bible. This Book is made up of 66 books, each written separately alhough some writers produced more than one of these books. The Book is inspired of God because it contains information that could only have come from God. For instance, who but God could give us the story of Creation? No one else was there until the creation was completed with Adam and Eve. They were not witnesses of what God had done. Even they could not relate to us any information about God's creating the heavens and the earth. Only God could tell us that ... and a lot of other things. Creation is only one example.

There is a cohesiveness to the Bible that seems contrary to the fact that it was written over a period of several hundred years, by men who never conferred with one another to "get their story straight". The Bible itself claims to have been written "by the will of God", not born out of the ambitions of men.

This Book is good for cleansing - for Jesus' words are contained in it and His words make us clean. God's words are "fit to eat" as well for the prophet Jeremiah said, "Thy words were found and I did eat them and ... they were the joy and rejoicing of my heart." God's Word is life to the soul- "hear, and your soul shall live." The Word of God is also light for the Psalmist said, "The entrance of Thy word giveth light."

We don't go through a day without washing, eating and using light to accomplish the activities of our day. Spending time in God's Word each day is equally necessary. If we neglect it, we get "dirty"; we are weakened as a person without food and we stumble about as if we were in complete darkness.

REMEMBER: Make God's Word part of your daily life and find "joy and rejoicing" for your heart.

BOOK OF LIFE

Books appear to be very important to God. He keeps a book about eternal matters. There is a record in heaven of the names of those who obey God although those who disobey are "blotted out" - erased from that book. This is called, "the Book of Life", and in it are listed those who have "overcome" in the name of Jesus.

- These are the faithful who continued to believe in spite of a world set contrary to God and all that is good (Rev. 20:4).

- These are the ones who refused to abandon their faith in God even in the face of torture and death.

The names listed there are announced aloud to God, the Father, and to all His angels. These are believers which bring joy to the heart of God, and they will be clothed in white when they stand before their King.

Has your name been listed in the Book of Life?

Joyfully, Jesus will list it there with the many others who have believed, and you will find joy as well by knowing that your name is written there. Little else on earth can bring such joy and peace to your heart. It means that your sins are forgiven and your soul is at peace with God. There is no condemnation or judgment waiting ahead for you! With your name written in the Lamb's Book of Life, you will spend eternity with our Eternal King and Savior, Jesus Christ, the Righteous One. His heavenly home will be yours and you will walk in the light of His glory forevermore. What a wonderful future there is for those whose names are written down in Heaven!

REMEMBER: Don't worry about the social register. Have your name listed in the Lamb's Book of Life!

BRIDE

"All brides are beautiful," they say. There is a lot of truth in this old saying and it has a lot to do with the beautiful clothes worn on this special day. Great planning and care go into the selection of a wedding dress and the accompanying finery. The fabric is usually one of great beauty; the design meant to enhance the beauty of even the loveliest of brides.

Many brides treasure their wedding dress through the years and some even see their daughters married in that same, precious dress. The men usually wear tuxedoes or formal dark suits. The mothers of the bride and groom select something lovely to wear to signify the significance of the vows that are to be exchanged on the wedding day. Our tradition is to make the finest clothes part of the wedding celebration.

In referring to our salvation, Isaiah uses the wedding finery to describe the celebration that takes place when we find our salvation in Jesus Christ. Isaiah says,

"He has clothed me with the robe of righteousness, as a bridegroom decketh himself with ornaments, and as a bride adorns herself with jewels."

The joy of their hearts on their wedding day is displayed outwardly in beautiful clothes. In the same way, the great joy of salvation causes us to wear righteousness as an outward sign of the celebration going on in our hearts. The experience is unforgettable. The memories are treasured for days to come.

When the Bible tells us that believers are the *"bride of Christ"*, it conveys the value He places on us and also the great joy He gets from sharing His life with us.

REMEMBER: Life with Christ is as unforgettable and as joyous as your wedding day!

CAIN

The first son born on earth was named Cain which means "acquisition" because Adam and Eve had acquired a son. Cain was a restless man, however, and boredom dogged his footsteps wherever he went.

When God asked Cain and Abel to bring a sacrifice, Cain proudly brought the results of his labor - beautiful fruit and produce he had cultivated. He saw as relatively unimportant his father's story of an animal who had been killed to cover him and Eve when they had sinned. He failed to understand that the sacrifice of a lamb was necessary in God's sight to make atonement for sin. He didn't acknowledge that "without the shedding of blood, there is no forgiveness for sin" (Lev. 17:11). Instead, he offered God the products of his own labor.

In spite of Cain's carelessness and wilfullness, he was crushed that Abel's gift was accepted while his offering was rejected. The resentment that came easily to his human heart welled up inside of this restless man and burned deep into his thoughts. It was all made worse because Abel raised the sheep he used for an offering while Cain would have had to go to his younger brother to get the lamb he needed for his sacrifice. It was more than Cain could swallow. He just wouldn't do it God's way. It meant humbling himself before his brother - no way!

All people everywhere are the same in God's eyes - He loves them all and does not glorify one and count another unworthy. All of us are invited to come to Him, however, we all must come according to His plan for our salvation. If we are proud in our attitudes toward one another, we are proud before God and He will not accept our pride.

REMEMBER: "Pride goes before destruction," and "The humble heart God will not despise."

CANKER

Here's another Bible word that has fallen into disuse today except to describe those painful sores we get in our mouths from time to time. If you've ever had one, the definition of "canker" is obvious to you. The sores rise as a lump under the skin only to erupt into a raw crater of pain which does not go away quickly. As is plain to the eye, it is related to the word "cancer" and from the Greek for "gangrene".

Paul told Timothy that "profane and vain babblings" bring ungodliness and "eat away like a canker" (II Tim. 2:16,17). James uses this word to describe the corrosion of the wealth of those who gain their riches by imposing misery on others, defrauding them of their rightful wages.

Jesus spoke of the wisdom of saving treasures in heaven where there is no canker to eat away at them instead of storing up treasure on earth. Not only can thieves rob earthly riches, but they can be eaten away by corruption - cankered. My father used to say that almost anyone can make money, but it takes a smart person to keep it! How true! How many people in your own acquaintance have lost their retirement, had their investments go bad, or been cheated out of all they had by an unscrupulous "con man". Even the smartest among us is subject to their schemes.

Proverbs puts it this way: "Riches certainly make themselves wings; they fly away like an eagle toward heaven" (Prov. 23:5). On the other hand, Jesus said that the good we do is permanent and cannot be taken from us nor eaten away by rust or moths. He advised us to spend our time and energy on things that will not fade away. He also knew that our hearts become attached to the things on which we expend ourselves.

REMEMBER: "Where your treasure is, there will your heart be also."

CHANGE

As long as there is life, there will be change. The Bible speaks of changing garments, changing behavior, changing seasons and changing money. It tells of spiritual changes and physical changes on earth, in heaven, in governments, in homes and in individuals. The most striking changes occur in people when they come to know God because "if any man be in Christ, he is a new creature" - changed! (II Cor. 5:17).

John Bunyan is one such example. People shied away from him because of his extreme profanity. They thought God might strike him on the spot for his terrible language. Yet, after he found Jesus as his Savior, he used his words to write "Pilgrim's Progress", a classic tale which has blessed the hearts of many through the years. What a change God can make in a life!

The man who founded the first rescue mission in the United States had been a derelict drunkard who would have murdered a man for the few dollars in his pocket in order to buy another drink. Meeting Jesus turned him from a drunken sot into a saint who cared for others living as he had lived in the past.

A man I knew had lost his business and, in the stressful period that followed, had lost his wife. They sold their house and divided the money - she went back to college to get her neglected teaching degree and he moved out of the state to start yet another business which failed. His son had moved with him, but he joined the military and left the man alone in an unfamiliar place - broke and discouraged. He borrowed money to go to school to learn to drive a big truck on cross country deliveries. While driving, he began to listen to sermon tapes and renewed his walk with the Lord. In time, his family was restored to him along with his dignity and his joy! He is a changed man!

REMEMBER: Believe in God and you'll believe in miracles.

CHEEK

Jesus spoke of being hit on the cheek in His Sermon on the Mount. He told us to turn the other cheek so the one who hit you on one side of the face, can hit you on the other one. Impossible, you say? (Matt. 5).

H. Vander Lugt of *Our Daily Bread* told of a Cambodian Christian named Ta Hum whose neighbors bribed a surveyor in order to take away half an acre of his land. He was angry at first and went out with a machete to cut down every living plant on that land. Convicted, he returned home without carrying out his plan. He felt God was asking him to turn the other cheek. The next morning, he went to his neighbors and offered them his house, too. The news of this unusual offer spread through the village and the chief was so impressed that he decided to look into the matter. He returned all of Ta Hum's land to him.

Not all cases of "turning the other cheek" have such storybook endings - such outcomes are not promised by God. Still, we are commanded to treat others in the manner in which we ourselves would like to be treated.

That means that we don't take advantage of our friends even when it is within our grasp. We leave the best portions for our family. We do a thorough job for the people who hire us to work for them. We not only tell the truth, we don't try to mislead others by what we say or fail to say. We pay our fair share and we don't complain about it - who wants to listen to that?

Obviously, such behavior is not very common. It is bound to cause people to wonder when they see us willingly giving up the advantage. They may even think that we are a bit like Christ!

REMEMBER: Turning the other cheek may turn others to Christ.

CHILDREN

"Be fruitful and multiply" God told Adam and Eve. Until recent years, the bearing of children was the one thing that gave women status above all else. Men looked upon their offspring as "olive plants around their table". Grandchildren are the "crown of old men" Solomon wrote in Proverbs.

Endearingly, Jesus called His followers "little children" and we should view children as those whom we love and care for "as a father" - or mother. Children are not only to be protected from harm, but they are to be trained for adulthood, living in strength and wisdom before God and man. Parents are the primary teachers and training their children is their responsibility. How the children mature is a sign of their faithfulness in training and reflects the love and care given them by their parents. Even when some children turn against the ways of their fathers, it is to be clear that such is an act of rebellion, not necessarily a sign of carelessness on the part of the parents.

Jesus loved children and called them to His side on many occasions (see Matt. 19:13 for an example). He used them as examples of the humility and trust needed to be a true follower of God. Their lack of cynicism made it easy for them to trust in Jesus. In their innocence, children can accept the love and care that Jesus offers without great fear and distrust. It seems hard for grown-ups to believe that God loves them and offers to care for them as a father cares for his children.

One man with a family of five boys became ill and no longer could work. He said, "I thought I had been taking care of my family, but I learned that God had been taking care of them ... and me ... all the time!"

REMEMBER: Let us become child-like in our faith, not childish in our behavior.

CHRONICLES

There are twelve books of history in the Old Testament. Two of them are called Chronicles and tell of the history of Judah from the death of King Saul to the Babylonian Captivity. These books begin by tracing the genealogies of many to David who was King. The title, "chronicles", then is fulfilled in this list of family names. Although these lists make for dry reading, each name has a story connected with that person's life and experience.

Such a person is Jabez who was "more honorable than his brethren." Jabez called on God to bless him "indeed" and to enlarge his borders. He asked that God be with him and keep him from evil, and God granted his requests. Jabez wanted more than an average life. He pleaded for God's special blessing.

When we find ambition burning in our souls, we need to turn to God and seek His blessing to make that ambition (and its outcome) a blessing to God and man. Too many who have ambition use it up on themselves and hurt others along the way instead of being above average to the glory of God. God gives His blessings willingly to those who come to Him asking with a pure heart without seeking to glorify themselves. In your family's "chronicle", does your life stand out as a sign of God's blessing?

It is plain to see that God thought the lives of simple people were important since He recorded stories in His Word. Each person mentioned had a relationship (good or bad) with God and He preserved their stories for us so that we can see how God deals with people. Everyone of us has a story to tell of how we met Jesus and what He has done in our lives since that memorable day. May ours be stories of His love, mercy and grace!

REMEMBER: History is "His story" ... and ours!

CHURCH

• A church is a building - and it is the people that gather inside.

• The church is a "mystery" which reveals the truth about God and about Jesus Christ, His Son. The church people are a family, irrevocably joined together by the life of Christ which sustains them all.

• The church is built by Jesus who claimed it as His own, and those who belong to Him labor in the work of the church with great joy. Those who belong to Jesus are so closely knit together, they are spoken of as a "body" - each one an integral part of the rest.

There is an order to the church, beginning with Jesus Christ as "the head over all things to the church" (Eph. 1:22). Then the rest of the believers fit together to make up this living body, the church of Jesus Christ. This is no denomination for it crosses all lines and surmounts all barriers. Those who have trusted in Christ are all part of the same body no matter what their nationality or heritage, no matter what their financial status, no matter what their education or training, no matter what their language or location. There is a universal bond that has reached across every classification of mankind to link hearts of believers everywhere.

Perhaps you have not yet given your heart to Jesus and become one of His. To everyone who believes, He gives "the power to become the sons of God, even to those who believe on His name." How simple ... yet how profound. Simply believe, and embark on the greatest adventure of your life.

REMEMBER: Trust Jesus today and you will be part of His church family forever.

COME

This little word is one of the first words a child learns. He uses it to communicate his desires and wishes. Every mother has heard her child say, "Come" as he started off in one direction or another. It is also part of longer words which gain their meaning primarily from the basic word.

"Overcome" is a form of the word which indicates a problem, a burden, a habit in which a herculean effort is needed to triumph. Jesus said, "Father ... lead us not into temptation, but deliver us from evil". That is overcoming! It necessitates that we COME to a new source of power to find the strength we need to overcome.

"Become" is another word which speaks to us of coming to a new source of power. How can one who is weak, weary, and wayward become anything better than he has been? Jesus said, "Come to ME" and when we come, "all things are become new" (II Cor. 5:17), and WE BECOME more than we ever dreamed.

While "come" is an invitation, it is also a command which requires a decision on our part. Will we obey Jesus' command and come to Him, or will we decide to refuse His offer? He doesn't tell us to come after we've cleaned up our lives or come when we think the time is right. In fact, there are no conditions given for us to come to Jesus except that He calls those who are "weary and heavy laden" (Matt. 11:28) so He can give them rest.

You may not feel the need to come to Jesus just now, but none of us gets through life without feeling loaded down with the cares of life at times. Why wait until you are in a deep pit of despair before you turn to Jesus. His invitation is open to you today!

REMEMBER: Jesus says, "Come" and that means NOW!

COMFORTER

The Greek language uses several words which are all translated "comforter" in English. The one that most interests us here is "parakletos" which means "one called alongside to help". In a Greek court of law, an attorney can be referred to as a "parakletos". This word was used as a name for Jesus Christ in I John 2:1,2 when it tells us that He pleads our case with the Father when we have sinned. Jesus reminds the Father that He has already paid the penalty for our sin. A comforter is much more than a sympathetic friend. This shows us that He is (as Webster's dictionary says) "one who imparts strength; one who assists".

"My little children, I am writing these things to you that you may not sin, and if anyone sins, we have an advocate (an attorney) with the Father, Jesus Christ the righteous" (I Jn. 2:1-2).

The Holy Spirit is also called "The Comforter" and His ministry to us is very intimate. We find the emphasis on the fact that He is "alongside" us, living in us, reminding us of God's truth. Sometimes we are unaware of the work of the Holy Spirit since His function is to witness of Jesus - not to draw attention to Himself, but a believer can be sure that He is at work in his life.

Without Christ, we are like a defendant standing before the court of heaven without an attorney to plead our case. Indeed, we have no case to plead without Jesus because we're guilty and nothing is left except for the judge to pronounce sentence and punish us. However, when we admit our sinfulness and look to Jesus for salvation by His blood, we are forgiven and the son of the judge becomes our attorney!

REMEMBER: Don't let your "case" come to trial without making sure you are represented by an attorney - Jesus Christ, the spotless Lamb of God.

CORINTH

The ancient city of Corinth stands today and the archeologist's spade is making it live again! Corinth was a great city in Paul's day - wealthy and abounding with "thinkers" and orators. With all the affluence came a great deal of dissipation and immorality in this industrial port city.

Henrietta Mears described Corinth as a city that "attracted great crowds of foreigners from the East and West. Their gods were gods of pleaure and lust. There was much culture and art as well. The city abounded in studies of language and schools of philosophy." As in most cities within the Roman Empire, there was a large group of Jews who held to Judaism in spite of the pagan worship of Venus which surrounded them.

It was into this city that the Apostle Paul came as a middle-aged man and he went to work as a tentmaker in order to earn his living. Unlike others, however, Paul pursued tentmaking only as a means of supporting his missionary work and he spent every free moment witnessing of Jesus in the synagogues. Later, Paul's letters to the church at Corinth focussed on the divisions and politics which he had found there. Many prided themselves on belonging to a more "spiritual" group than any other, so the thrust of Paul's letters was on Christian conduct. His letters, which we know as the books of First and Second Corinthians, express Paul's grief and indignation over the unspiritual and immoral condition of the church.

How easy it is to get caught up in the activities that surround us and forget that God is interested in the affairs of humans and He cares very much how we treat one another. He is not impressed with our position! He seeks the humble heart.

REMEMBER: "Be ye steadfast, unmovable, always abounding in the work of the Lord."

CORINTHIANS

There are two letters by that same name. The theme of the second book is the subject of apostolic authority. It portrays Jesus as a Savior who is sufficient for all believers. Since Paul was unsure of how well they had accepted the rebukes of his first letter, Paul sent the second letter with Titus to get a firsthand assessment of the Church at Corinth.

Paul had heard that most of the people had accepted his teaching in a spirit of humility. Still, there were those who questioned Paul's right to claim that he was an Apostle since he was not one of the original twelve. This brought about the teaching in Second Corinthians. To convince the people of his apostleship, Paul told the history of what had happened to him through the years in his service for Christ. He had refrained from doing so before in order to avoid sounding like he was bragging.

Paul also shared the frustration of having prayed for so many who were healed and restored to full strength, only to find that his own physical limitations were not restored. He finally learned that God's "grace is sufficient ... His strength is made perfect in weakness."

In this book, we have the three aspects of salvation outlined for us:

- PAST - we are saved from the penalty of our sins,

- PRESENT - we are saved from the power of sin so we can live for Christ,

- FUTURE - we will be saved from the presence of sin when Jesus comes again.

REMEMBER: "If any man be in Christ, he is a new creature ... all things are become new" (II Cor. 5:17).

DANIEL

This was the name of an outstanding man who lived about 600 B.C., and this name holds within it the name of God. "Elohim", "El Shaddai", and many other names make it clear that the name of DaniEL is a reference to God. It means, "God is my judge". Daniel took a stand for God before everyone - even the most powerful king of history, saying, "You are not the final authority - God is my judge." Daniel's life proved that God had the final word, no matter which king was in control (Dan. 1-12).

As a young man, Daniel was torn from his home and his country and carried off to Babylon to serve the king there. He was taken along with the best of all the young men of Israel. These men were all handsome, intelligent and (so the king thought) trainable in the ways of the Babylonians. Surely, such youths would welcome the opportunity to enter the king's court and learn from the best teachers of the land. They gave Daniel a pagan name which never became his real name in God's sight. That name replaced God with one of their pagan gods. The problem arose in that Daniel and his friends had been too well trained in the faith of their fathers to fall prey to an idolatrous religion. They chose to obey God even if it cost them their lives. God preserved their lives and they stood out above all others.

Babylon was a city that was in its zenith during the days of Daniel. King Nebuchadnezzar had conquered the world that then was, and he built a palace, a city, and a garden which have remained in history as wonders of the world, but even this great king was not worthy of the worship that belongs to God. Daniel was thrown to the lions for remaining faithful to the true God and God delivered Daniel.

REMEMBER: "Let all those who put their trust in [God] rejoice ... because [He] defends them" (Ps. 5:11).

DAY

In the beginning of creation, there was no day or night. The Bible tells us that God began counting time ("In the beginning") when He created the heavens and the earth, and He defined and limited the day by light. Even now, the dictionary says that day is "a period of light between one night and the next." We know that a day and a night are required for the Earth to complete one full rotation on its axis.

God also created and set in place the sun to rule the day and to divide it from the night. Within the functioning of the sun and moon, God implanted signs, seasons, days and years. Through the centuries, God has kept the heavenly bodies in their place and He told us to count on them "as surely as day follows night". To Noah, God said that day and night would not cease "as long as the earth remaineth". Yet, there will come a day when "day and night will come to an end" (Job 26:10). Peter warns that "the heavens shall pass away with a great noise, and the elements shall melt with fervent heat, the earth also ..." (II Peter 3:10).

Then, John tells us of seeing "a new heaven and a new earth: for the first heaven and the first earth were passed away" (Rev. 21:1). When that day comes, there will no longer be day or night, but Jesus, the Lamb of God, will be the light of the city where believers will live. There are many "daily days", "one-after-the-other" days by which we measure our lives. The Psalmist saw the importance of each one of these humdrum days and prayed, *"So teach us to number our days that we may apply our hearts to wisdom"* (Ps. 90:12). That's the secret! Our lives are worth living because of the mercy of the Lord - our joy is to "apply our hearts" to understand Him!

REMEMBER: "The mercy of the Lord is from everlasting to everlasting to them that fear Him."

DEACON

Only five times in all of Scripture do we find this word. Yet, many churches today use this name for the leaders of their church. A lofty picture is given of the lifestyle for such leaders. Deacons are to be living pictures of the best and highest in the Christian life. In agreeing to serve as a deacon, or in voting to elect a person as deacon, we need to know if his life presents the best possible "image of Christ" in human flesh. So it was that Paul told Timothy that those who lead must be tested - observed - to see if they are "blameless".

Since men only were the first deacons, their wives were also to be "faithful in all things", and their children under control. Paul promised that those men who served well as deacons would be honored and would find boldness to carry on the faith of Jesus Christ. We wisely use the term "to serve as a deacon" because the word comes from a designation for servants meaning both slaves and hired help, and it carries the connotation "to minister". When the apostles were overloaded and unable to minister to the needs of the widows, deacons were selected to carry out this responsibility. The deacons literally served food at the tables and they were set apart and dedicated for this work of seeing that all the church members had what they needed.

This practical, daily ministering was taken care of by men who were *"full of the Holy Spirit and wisdom"* and they were installed with prayer and great dedication. It was no small responsibility to see that the needs of all the people were met, and it was given to those who were qualified spiritually.

Does it seem mundane to see that people are fed? It required the best credentials to serve in this way.

REMEMBER: "My God shall supply all your need, according to His riches in glory."

DEATH

We think of death as a life ended, a soul departed, but by itself, death only means separation. True, physical death is a soul separated from its physical home, the body in which it stayed for a while, but the soul itself does not come to an end. Another separation which is called "death" is the spiritual separation of the sinner from our righteous God, but when the sinner finds the life of God, he is dead to sin - separated from sin. We are either "alive to God" by believing in Christ, or we are "dead in trespasses and sins". When we are alive to God, we are dead to sin and to our self-centered way of thinking and living. That's what Paul talked about when he said,

"Christ liveth in me: and the life which I now live in the flesh, I live by the faith of the Son of God" (Gal. 2:20).

How different Paul would have been if he had put comfort ahead of serving the Lord! What if Paul had felt too tied down with his responsibilities in Tarsus to leave and travel all those missionary miles? No, Paul was set on one thing - being a disciple of Christ at any cost.

When Julius Caesar invaded the shores of Britain with his Roman legions, he knew it would take an all-out effort to gain the victory he wanted. After his men had gone ashore and climbed the Cliffs of Dover, he commanded them to turn and look back at the ships in which they had come to those shores. They were horrified to see every ship ablaze leaving them no possible retreat. They had to go forward, and they had to conquer that new land.

REMEMBER: To His disciples, Jesus said, "Whosoever ... forsaketh not all that he hath cannot be my disciple" (Luke 14:33).

DELIVER

Here is a word that can be used for everything from depositing a letter in the proper mailbox to the arrival of a newborn baby, but however it is used, it must have an object - in these cases, the letter and the baby. There is always something that is delivered. The definitions include "to set free from", "to transfer the possession of", "to hand over to another", and "to convey goods to a destination and leave them there".

In the story of Shadrach, Meshach and Abednego (Dan. 3), we find three young men who were in a terrible plight. They had angered the most powerful king on earth and he was about to throw them into the fiery furnace. They did not know what God's will was for them - sometimes believers have been killed for their faith. These young men were willing to die for their faith if that was God's plan for them. On the other hand, they believed with all their hearts that God was able to deliver them. They knew that their King was stronger than the earthly King Nebuchadnezzar whose wrath they had aroused. They believed in deliverance. They were so bold that they said to the king, "Our God is able to deliver us from the fiery furnace". They went on record as believing in the deliverance that God could give.

Even so, the deliverance came to them in a way they had not expected for they were thrown into the fiery furnace which was so hot it burned to death those who threw them into the flames. Once inside, however, they found that only the ropes that bound them burned and they walked around in the flames - but not just three, there were four men in the fire! The king said that the fourth man looked like the "Son of God".

REMEMBER: The "new birth" delivers us from the fires of hell and, by faith, we can be delivered from the power of sin in our lives.

DEMAS

We first hear of this man when he joined Paul and Luke to travel with them in their missionary journies. He seemed to be happy to travel and work with these men of God, but things often became difficult and dangerous. They were not well received, and sometimes they were beaten and stoned. Was this what turned Demas away? Not really.

Paul wrote that Demas left him because he loved "this present world" (II Tim. 4:10). It appears that Demas wanted "the good life" and had gotten a better offer than roaming the countryside with Paul. Demas means "popular" and he was undoubtedly a good-looking young man - lots of potential. It seemed a shame to waste that on a life of rejection and persecution. Then, too, besides the position in life that he might achieve, Demas knew there were more comfortable places to be than those he had with Paul. A secure home, a steady job, a loving family and friends were the things that Demas wanted out of life - nothing wrong with that! These are all good things unless they become more precious to us than God. Jesus said,

"Love not the world, neither the things that are in the world. If any man love the world, the love of the Father is not in him. ... the pride of life is not of the Father but is of the world. The world passes away and the lusts thereof; but he that doeth the will of God abideth forever" (I Jn. 2:15-17).

There is no doubt that it is costly to be faithful to Christ and accept the hard times as well as the blessings; however, God requires faithfulness in those who serve Him and He promises rewards to those who endure.

REMEMBER: "Be not weary in well doing, for in due season, we shall reap if we faint not" (Gal. 6:9).

DEUTERONOMY

The first five books of the Bible form a unit called, The Pentateuch and they tell the story of mankind from creation through the years of leadership given by Moses. Deuteronomy is the last of these books and is a farewell to the Children of Israel from Moses who had led them for many years. It is a review of all that God had done and Moses' last chance to add anything he might have forgotten before. Moses was forbidden by God to enter the Promised Land and he stood on Mount Nebo looking into that land with great longing.

On a trip to the Middle East, I was once denied entry into Israel because of a 48-hour tourist law. That time period was completed on a Friday evening, so then I was banned until the Jewish Sabbath was over. While waiting, I decided to go to Mount Nebo as Moses had and I could glimpse the Dead Sea and the promised Land from the same place where Moses stood. Unlike Moses, I was eventually allowed to enter Israel while Moses died within sight of his goal.

Moses was denied the fulfillment of his goal because of his disobedience to God - a breach of the covenant God had made with him. God had offered blessings beyond imagination in return for the obedience of the Children of Israel. He brought them out of the land of Egypt and gave them their own land which was very good. God also made clear that their loyalty was required in return. Failure to meet the terms of the covenant was to bring curses on them so that they would return to worship God. Their choice was clear, yet they forgot from time to time in spite of all the wonderful works of God on their behalf. How much better it is to remember God's goodness and His mercy to us.

REMEMBER: "I have set before you life and death, blessing and cursing; therefore, choose life" (Deut. 30:19,20).

DOOR

This everyday word means both the entryway into a building and the panel which blocks entry and secures the building from outsiders. The Bible speaks of Noah and "the door of the ark". Abraham is said to have been sitting in "the door of the tent" in the middle of the day. Also mentioned is "the door of the tabernacle" where worshippers entered with their offerings. Jesus spoke of doors, too. He said that believers are to pray "with the door shut".

The shepherds of Jesus' day built a round pen for their sheep to find protection at night, but it had no door. When darkness began to fall, the shepherd drove his sheep into the pen. He might have to go after a wayward sheep and carry it on his shoulders to get all of his sheep into the pen. Then, the shepherd himself lay down across the doorway and he became the door -the protective barrier between his sheep and the wild creatures who emerged from their dens at night. Just so, Jesus said that He is the door of His sheep and no one enters without His knowledge and permission. He promised to keep them from destruction.

In Revelation 3 and 4, three doors are seen. Outside the closed door of the Church of Laodicea, Jesus is pictured - standing and knocking - waiting for them to open the door and let Him come in. To the Church at Philadelphia, Jesus said, "I have set before you an open door, and no one can shut it". He was giving them an opportunity to witness to unbelievers at home and abroad. The third door was left open as an invitation to the Apostle John to "Come up here" and take a look at heavenly things which are to come.

REMEMBER: Jesus said, "I am the door; by Me if any enter in, he shall be saved" and others hear of Him through those of us who believe.

EAR

A most important connection with the world around us is the sounds that reach us through our ears. This relatively small part of the body and its tiny bones give us a major tool for life and communication. In Bible times, the phrase, "inclined his ear" was often used to indicate that the hearer was really listening. God "bowed down His ear" - He was interested, and paid close attention to their prayers. Shakespeare wrote, "Friends, Romans and countrymen, lend me your ears." He wanted their full attention.

• When Old Testament priests were consecrated, blood was placed on their ears to cleanse and dedicate their hearing to God.

• When a leper was cleansed, the priest took some of the blood from his offering and put it on the tip of his ear.

• A slave who chose to stay with his master of his own free will had his ear pierced with an awl.

What lessons these examples have for us! We, too, have need of the blood of Jesus Christ to dedicate our ears to hear His Word and to forsake the sounds of sin.

• When we are cleansed from sin as the leper was cleansed of his spots, we are washed in Jesus' blood.

• When we give ourselves to God - willingly pledging our loyalty to Him, our hearing shows a marked change.

James points out, though, that hearing the truth by itself, is not enough - we must obey and live by the truth we have learned. Our ears can be ready at all times to hear God's voice as we study His Word and listen for that "still, small voice".

REMEMBER: The dearest message we can ever hear is this: "Jesus saves".

EBENEZER

This is the name of a town where the Children of Israel camped before a battle with the Philistines. They fought and when they won, Samuel put up a stone and called it Ebenezer, "a stone of help". It was a memorial to God's help and faithfulness to His children. It is a good thing to remember what God has done for us. It warms our hearts and encourages our souls.

Often in the middle of a trial, we don't see and understand what God is doing. Only later can we look back and see that He was indeed guiding, leading and controlling the circumstances and the outcome of our difficulties. God's promises which we find in the Bible are like Ebenezer - they are stones to help us remember God's goodness ... past and future (Psalm 103).

- He's promised to feed and clothe us.
- He will love us forever.
- He's promised never to leave us nor forsake us.
- He will give us strength in times of trouble.
- He hears us when we pray.

A great Bible teacher, Dr. James M. Gray, had been ill and part of his convalescence was a sea voyage. When the time came, however, he couldn't go because he had developed yet another physical problem. He felt frustrated and penned in by the four walls of his bedroom. The newspaper soon revealed God's reason for denying him that relief - the ship on which he was to have sailed had been sunk and the passengers lost. God had further need of him here on earth; He had spared his life for His purposes.

REMEMBER: If God leads you along stony paths, He will provide you with strong shoes.

ECCLESIATES

"The words of the preacher" is the opening of this Bible book. Ecclesiastes means "preacher" or "orator" and Solomon wrote these words when he was older. Psalms and Proverbs come from prior years. These are the conclusions that Solomon reached concerning life - his observations and deductions. Solomon decided that life is vanity - emptiness. He found nothing that satisfied his soul or made his life seem worthwhile. This was the conclusion of the wisest man who ever lived!

Solomon had been given the throne of David in peaceful security, not enduring the bitter battles and strife with which David had come to that throne. His life was easy, and he had riches, honor and power, yet he found them all empty of joy and satisfaction. *"Vanity, vanity, all is vanity"*, he cried.

Solomon could see that God had *"made everything beautiful in its time"*. He saw the patterns of life which most of us follow. He had no better idea, but even his great wealth, his achievements and his wisdom did not fill the emptinessof his heart.

It has been said that everyone has a "God-shaped" emptiness in his heart and until we find God and fellowship with Him, we ache with that emptiness. Solomon, too, came to that conclusion for his final exhortation is:

> *"Fear God and keep His commandments, for this is the whole duty of man. For God shall bring every work into judgment, with every secret thing, whether it be good or evil" (Eccl.12:13,14).*

What's your goal? Will it satisfy you when you achieve it?

REMEMBER: All of Solomon's blessings left him still in need of God.

EMMANUEL

This was the name given to Jesus in Isaiah's prophecy, 800 years before His birth in Bethlehem. Matthew tells us that it means "God with us" and surely, God was with us while Jesus walked the Earth.

John put it this way:

"The Word was God ... and the Word was made flesh and dwelt among us" (Jn. 1:14).

Paul said that *"God was manifest in the flesh."*

One Christmas Eve, a family went off to church without the father since he was not a believer. Alone on the farm, snow falling outside, he heard an unusual noise and went to investigate. He traced the noise to the barn and he saw a flock of birds flying toward the barn door, trying to get out of the storm. The farmer opened the door wider, but the birds were frightened of him and his lantern and still wouldn't enter. He wished he might communicate with them and his train of thought took him to the conclusion that he would have to become one of them in order to lead them to safety. Church bells reminded him that it was Christmas Eve and suddenly, he saw the light - God's light! He saw that God had come in human flesh in order to communicate with us the message of salvation and safety - how to be rescued from the ravages of sin.

Jesus opened His arms wide as He hung on the Cross, but they were wide open to welcome us to Himself, too. Over and over again, He says to us, "Come unto Me, and I will give you rest for your souls." The farmer came to Jesus on that Christmas Eve as he knelt in the snow. Won't you come to Jesus, too?

REMEMBER: God became a man for a while, so that we can be God's children for eternity.

ENOCH

After Cain killed Abel, it appears that he made his peace with God for he named his firstborn son Enoch which means "consecrated". Jared's son, another Enoch, begot him a grandson whose name was Methusaleh. Although it is said that Abraham *"walked before God"*, it is said of Enoch and Noah that they *"walked with God"*. Enoch walked so closely with God that he went directly to heaven - he was *"translated that he should not see death"* (Gen. 5:24).

I heard of a young father who took his son to the beach. The boy constantly lagged behind, stopping here and there. "What are you doing, son?" asked his mother. The delighted child said,"I'm stepping where Daddy stepped." Every child follows the steps of his parents and perhaps Enoch decided to walk with God so that he would leave footprints leading to the Heavenly Father. He wanted Methusaleh and his other children to walk in his footsteps and move ever closer to God. Enoch's desire became a pattern for his life. He knew that this meant taking one step at a time, a succession of steps toward spiritual maturity. *"Enoch walked with God: and he was not; for God took him"*. God by-passed death for Enoch and we find that death loses its sting when we walk with God for death is the gate by which we reach greater fellowship with Him (Heb. 11:5,6).

We are instructed that since we have received Jesus as Savior, we are to *"walk in Him: rooted and built up in Him, and stablished in the faith."*

Walking is a daily activity—not a single leap into space. Mountaintop experiences are wonderful, but we must walk the valleys one step at a time (Jude 14).

REMEMBER: We can walk all the way hand in hand with Jesus to guide us and to stay with us so we're never alone.

EPAPHRAS

Paul names many of his helpers and associates in his writings. Epaphras is one of those who worked with Paul and was his friend. He worked with Paul in the church at Colosse and, perhaps, was even the founder of that church. Epaphras was also in jail with Paul for he calls him his *"fellowprisoner"*. Epaphras also travelled with Paul, but his heart remained in Colosse for he prayed for them earnestly and fervently - Paul called it *"working hard for you"* (Col. 4:12-13).

Evidently, Epaphras had taught the people of Colosse well because their faith was plain to see by their loving actions toward other Christians. We learn by means of the Colossians that those who receive the Gospel become Christians in character which grows and develops from the time the Gospel is heard and believed. Epaphras had taught them and their well-being was still his chief concern. They were blessed to have such a shepherd as Epaphras.

Even more, when he was not with them, he talked about them in such a way that his hearers were made to love them, too, and to pray for them almost as fervently as Epaphras did. This good man is an example to all of the great blessing we can be by bringing others to Jesus Christ and nurturing them in God's truth. There is a great deal of spiritual insight and understanding that many never come to see without this kind of **care and prayer** from a loving, faithful friend. Today, some call it "friendship evangelism" but it came naturally to the heart of Epaphras. The love of God that he had received, he longed to share with the people he loved. Then they became so dear to him that he could not spend a day without thinking of them and praying for them.

REMEMBER: The love we have for our Unseen Friend is made plain by the love we show to our earthly friends.

EPHESIANS

A city in what is now Turkey was called Ephesus - a metropolis where Paul went to preach the Gospel. Later, he wrote a letter to the people of the church there for many had believed in Christ in that great city. This letter contains some of the most descriptive passages in the Bible concerning our faith and our walk in Christ.

• Paul wrote of the blessings of being a believer and his words speak of *"all spiritual blessings"* and *"heavenly places"*.

• Paul tells of *"grace"* and *"peace"* from God, the Father, and from Jesus Christ.

• Paul says that believers are *"adopted in Christ"*, *"accepted in the Beloved"*, *"redeemed and forgiven in Christ"*, our lives are *"centered in Christ"*, we inherit great riches in Christ, we are *"glorified in Christ"*, in Him we have wisdom, hope, power, life, exaltation, growth, and stature.

• We receive His promises, God's wisdom, access to the throne of heaven, and ... everything in Christ Jesus. The only area in which we are to go to excess is in allowing the Holy Spirit to invade every corner of our our lives. *"Be not drunk with wine, but be filled with the Spirit,"* Paul writes. Wine permeates the entire system, but for believers, the Holy Spirit is to filter through every area of our lives instead (Eph. 5:18).

This letter closes with imagery of a suit of armor for the soldier of God. The armor is God's and we are to put it on in order to be prepared to *"stand ... as good soldiers"*. Our Commander is sending us into a battle of faith.

REMEMBER: "Be strong and of good courage. Be not afraid, neither be dismayed, for the Lord, thy God, He it is that doth go with thee" (Josh. 1:6).

ESTHER

The name of this beautiful woman means "star" as though it were pronounced "E - STAR". She was born in ancient Persia where her people were slaves to those who had taken them captive many years before. They had removed only the best and brightest from their homeland (Israel) so she came from those who had been strongest and handsomest among her people.

When King Ahasueras sent for his queen, Vashti, she defied his command and refused to come. Her punishment was that she would never again be called by the king. Instead, a beauty contest was held to select a new queen. Esther's uncle, Mordecai, served the king in Shushan, and had raised his orphaned niece there. Esther was noticed and was taken to the palace along with the other young unmarried women where they were given beauty creams and make-up to prepare themselves for the king for twelve months. When he saw Esther, the king loved her more than any of the others.

A crisis arose when Haman, an enemy of Mordecai and all the Jews, persuaded the king to allow them to be killed on a certain day and they were not to defend themselves. Little did the king know that his queen and his closest advisor (Mordecai) were Jews! Mordecai pleaded with Esther to go to the king and seek help. Taking her life in her hands, she went before this powerful king and found favor with him and defense for her people.

Haman saw that the king was angry with him and he fell at Esther's feet pleading for his life. The king thought Haman was attacking her, and commanded that he be put to death. So it was Haman, not Mordecai, who was put to death. Never again did the Persians dare to persecute the Jews of that day.

REMEMBER: Salvation is from God. He is our sure defense.

EXODUS

Seventeen centuries before Christ was born in Bethlehem, the Children of Israel were slaves in Egypt. They had gone there when Joseph was "Prime Minister" as the members of his family alone, but in the intervening years, they had become a great nation within a nation.

Still, they were slaves and their taskmasters were cruel and hard. The Jews longed for the homeland that God had given them. Through unusual and amazing circumstances, Moses was appointed by God to lead them out - to exit from Egypt; hence, the name "The Exodus". There were more than a half million men, plus their wives and families. Their departure could hardly remain a secret!

God in His wisdom sent ten plagues to soften the attitude of the Pharoah whose oppression made the lives of the Children of Israel so miserable. Each plague presented a major problem to the king. Frogs covering the land made his people as miserable as he had been making his slaves. Blood in the rivers instead of water, put the Egyptians in a state of crisis - they could not live without water! Still, nothing broke the king's hold on the Israelites until God took the firstborn son from every household by the Angel of Death. The Jews, too, would have lost their oldest son if they had not obeyed the command of God to kill a spotless lamb, roast and eat the meat, having placed the blood of the lamb on the sides and top of their front doors. Then God led them out of slavery into His Promised Land. Our lamb is Jesus, spotless Lamb of God who takes away the slavery to sin of the whole world if we will accept His sacrifice for ourselves.

REMEMBER: Jesus said, "I am the Life", and "I am come that they might have life, and that they might have it more abundantly" (Jn. 10:10).

EYES

We all know that we see with our eyes, but the Bible speaks of having the *"eyes of our understanding opened"*, and this has a deeper meaning. The Serpent told Eve that if she would eat of the tree which God had forbidden, her *"eyes would be opened"* and she would know *"good and evil"* - she would *"be as the gods"*. So it was that the Age of Innocence ended in Eve's desire to be like God and her willingness to disobey His command in order to gain something more for herself (Gen. 3:5).

Adam loved her and chose to follow suit rather than to obey God's command. The new awareness of themselves and God that came with their disobedience caused them to use fig leaves in an effort to make themselves acceptable to God. God would not let them hide from Him and He gave them protection in the form of skins from the animal that He killed for them. His teaching was, *"Without the shedding of blood, there is no forgiveness for sin"*.

Adam and Eve could not save themselves from their sin. God provided the salvation they needed and so a great truth was given so that by the *"eyes of our understanding"* we can know that we need to find salvation by going God's way (Eph. 1:8).

In the New Testament, many times people with blind eyes came to Jesus seeking to have their sight restored to them. Jesus healed them all - *"their eyes were opened"*. We identify with those whose physical eyes were blind because our spiritual eyes are blinded by sin and cannot be opened without the healing touch of Jesus Christ. We cannot understand the truth that Jesus taught without His work in us to open *"the eyes of our understanding"* (Luke 24:45).

REMEMBER: "From whence cometh my help? My help cometh from the Lord, who made heaven and earth" (Ps. 121:1).

EZEKIEL

This name is a word, a man, an Old Testament book and a self-contained truth. EL at the end of this word is the name of God incorporated into the name of a man. The first part means "strength".

After Daniel had been taken away from Israel as a hostage, Ezekiel followed - a prisoner of the Babylonians, conquerors of his homeland. He lived as a captive for twenty-seven years, but at all times, Ezekiel was in the hand of God. God had a purpose in his captivity which Ezekiel was to explain to his people. Israel had been guilty of great sin and **rebellion** against God and although God destroyed other nations who had turned against Him, He preserved Israel - but not without punishment. The captivity was designed to bring God's people to the **realization** that God is God and they were not to worship idols in the place of God. Shadrach, Meshach and Abednego went into the fiery furnace rather than worship the king. Daniel faced the lions in their den rather than to bow down to the king. Idolatry hasn't been a problem with the Jews since the days of Ezekiel.

Responsibility is one of the main themes of Ezekiel's preaching for each of us must surely answer to God for our lives and for the lives of others if we see they are headed in the wrong direction and fail to warn them. **Recruitment** is another theme which Ezekiel teaches. He spoke of God seeking for those who would warn mankind of impending destruction.

Resurrection is another theme of Ezekiel for God promised to bring that dead nation to life again. God promised to save them - for His own name's sake ... to bring honor to His name.

REMEMBER: God holds us responsible, too, and He seeks to recruit us to do His will. The promise of resurrection is offered to us as well ... our Redeemer lives!

EZRA

Like Ezekiel, Ezra was a captive in a foreign land, and God had a purpose for his life, too. After seventy years of captivity, God called on Ezra to lead the first group of captives back to their homeland. As you might guess, his name means "help".

Nebuchadnezzar, the king who had conquered the Israelites, was gone and Artaxerxes became the ruler. His heart was softened by the pleas of Ezra to be allowed to return home and begin to rebuild their land. At last, these proud, wayward people had fulfilled God's punishment for their sins and restoration was begun. Ezra secured papers from the king with which to get timbers and supplies he would need, but he had to persuade his own people that God had once again decided to bless them and their land.

Their sins had brought them into the place of abject slavery where they had no choices, no freedom - nothing but disgrace. They were slaves, but God had not forgotten those He loved. Instead, God gave them favor with the King of Persia and they were allowed to return and to rebuild their cities. Ezra led the people in confessing their sins and in challenging them to live lives that would be pleasing to God. God's people were to separate themselves from sin and from the people who indulged in sin so that they would be different and distinct from the nations around them.

The spiritual lesson here is clear for we are servants to sin without our God. We are helpless for we don't have the strength to stand against it, and although God allows us to suffer because of our sin, He does not forget us.

REMEMBER: "If we confess our sin, God is faithful and just to forgive us our sin and to cleanse us from all unrighteousness" (I Jn. 1:9).

FACE

This word is found among the first verses of the Bible ..."*the face of the deep ... the face of the waters*". After Cain killed his brother, God pronounced his punishment and he cried,

"Thou hast driven me from the face of the earth: and from Thy face shall I be hid" (Gen. 4:13,14).

We see here two meanings of the word "face" - one is a surface, the other a countenance. Cain believed there was no place left for him on the surface of the earth, but his greatest anguish was that God was turning away from him.

David, too, felt that anguish when he had sinned and God turned His back on him. David sought the face of God once again and said, *"Hide not thy face far from me"* (Ps. 27:9). Even though God is a spirit, the heart of mankind longs for His fellowship and we think of that communication in terms of His face. God Himself commands us to seek His face and we respond in prayer and study of God's Word to find His blessing and friendship.

The blessing God gave to Moses for Aaron and his sons was, *"The Lord make His face to shine upon thee ... the Lord lift up His countenance upon thee, and give thee peace"* (Num.6:22-27).

So fellowship and peace are linked with the face of God. In the New Testament, Jesus told His disciples that when they had seen Him, they had seen God, the Father, yet Jesus' face was the face of a man. We, too, must seek the face of God in Jesus Christ for He is the one who reveals God to us—in Jesus we see the face of God.

REMEMBER: Let's face it! There is no way to see God's face or to find fellowship with Him except through faith in Jesus Christ.

FAIL

What bitterness there is in this word. Redundantly, we say someone is "an utter, complete failure", but this is repetitious for to fail means utter, complete inability to do what we have set out to do. There is no such thing as "a partial failure" for if we have done a thing at all (no matter how poorly), we have not failed.

Jesus came to earth teaching men that He is the Son of God and His death on the cross demonstrates His failure to convince men of that fact. He was discredited by the leadership of established religion, rejected by society and forsaken by His friends. When Jesus died, His failure seemed complete.

A great deal of kindness is done in the name of doing good. We pray God's blessing on projects designed to glorify people. Money given to God is poured out in the name of goodness but without God's blessing and satisfaction. Seeming to be good, these things fail ... while seeming to fail, Jesus did good to all men. Adam and Eve failed and it is called, "The Fall of Man". Lucifer, the archangel, failed and his pride caused him to fall from heaven in disgrace. We all fail for "*All have sinned and come short of the glory of God*" (Rom. 3:23).

Early Christian martyrs were called upon to face lions who tore them to bits, to be burned at the stake at the hands of godless men, to be sawn in two or thrown to wild animals to the shouts of a bloodthirsty crowd. Was this failure? So it seemed. However, just as Jesus' apparent failure was turned to success when He was raised from the dead, so these martyrs gave their lives - but not in vain. The name of Christ was lifted up by their faithfulness, and theirs was success, not failure (Heb. 11).

REMEMBER: God's thoughts are not our thoughts, and His ways are not our ways. His successes sometimes appear to be failures in the eyes of men.

FAMILY

In spite of current controversy, a family is a group of related people, objects or things having some features in common. God claims all believers as part of His family and we have His features implanted within us. All the people of the earth are called a "family" of humanity and we have many features in common - both visible and invisible. The traits of our bodies as well as the traits of our personalities have features in common.

Throughout history, God has made clear that the family is a unit that is vital to Him and to His plans. Gideon is a great example of the importance God places on family for when God began to cleanse the nation of Israel from the curse of the Midianites, He sent Gideon to his father's house to throw down the altar to Baal there. The superstitions and idolatry of the family were to be destroyed first (Judges 6).

Many that Jesus healed were instructed to go home and tell their families and friends about the great thing that God had done for them. Barbara Bush was right when she declared, "It is not what happens in the White House, but what happens at YOUR house that makes the difference for America." Like Gideon, we must throw out the idolatry and superstition that creep into our homes, unwisely and unwelcome. God will not bless our nation until we restore the faith of our families.

Abraham sought ten righteous in the city of Sodom to turn away God's wrath, but as Lot was forced to flee before God's destruction fell on that city, so we often must escape or we will be punished along with the unrighteous. Shall we not restore our families to honoring God and His Word before destruction comes upon our nation?

REMEMBER: "The children of the righteous will be delivered" (Prov. 11:21).

FELLOWSHIP

Some clever person has said that "fellowship" is "two fellows in the same ship", yet it has come to mean more than saying, "We're all in the same boat". There is a warmth and a closeness which we impute to the word "fellowship" that wasn't necessarily present in the original meaning.

Paul wrote that he was thankful for the people in Philippi for their "fellowship in the furtherance of the gospel" because they took part in his work of spreading the Gospel. These people had sent financial support to Paul and his fellow workers to enable them to preach the Gospel to those who had not heard. Paul counted this as full participation in his ministry - "fellowship" !

In the fellowship of believers (as we now count fellowship), there is an intimacy which includes confessing our faults to one another, praying together, meeting together for preaching of the Gospel and encouraging one another to love and good works.

More importantly, we are to maintain our fellowship with God at all times. Like a branch growing from the vine, we are to be imbedded into Christ in such a way that we can constantly receive sustenance from Him. He is the source of our life. This picture makes it clear that fellowship isn't just something nice we can take part in when we feel like it - it is the essential nature of our relationship with God. Just as a man is known by the company he keeps, so we are known as Christians when we are in fellowship with Jesus Christ. His life in us makes us like Him instead of being like we used to be. We bear His fruit (love, joy, peace, et al) when His life is in us. That's what Paul meant when he said, *"I am crucified with Christ; nevertheless, I live, yet not I, but Christ lives in me"* (Gal. 2:20).

REMEMBER: If fellowship means "two fellows in the same ship" make sure that your companion is Jesus Christ.

FIGHT

As much as mothers tell their children not to fight, we find in God's Word that we ARE to fight. Paul speaks of fighting "the good fight" so we cannot conclude that fighting is bad. Of course, mothers try to keep their children from taking advantage of one another while God's fight is a fight of faith (II Tim. 4:7).

As believers, we struggle against sin and wrong, and we fight to uphold the truth of God so that all may hear. Moreover, there is a way in which to fight which makes us effective and not wasting motion like a shadow boxer. We're not just to go through the motions of fighting, we are actually to fight and fight well - trying to win.

Our opponent is the devil (I Peter 5:8) and he is like a roaring lion, trying to conquer us. He is seeking to win with all his might. After spending his life engaging the enemy of our souls, Paul believed that he had *"fought the good fight ... finished my course ... kept the faith"*. God had laid out a course of action for Paul to follow and Paul believed that he had completed God's will for his life - this was *"fighting the good fight"*. Paul then looked for his reward from heaven. Paul had confronted sin and wickedness and had remained faithful to His Savior.

Christians today seem to believe that confrontation is bad - it isn't "nice". We seek peace at any price, but that is not God's way. Jesus pointed out that He came to separate the closest of relatives if one was a believer and the other was not. This implies that each has taken a stand as a believer or as unbeliever, as the case may be. God expects believers to let others know where they stand.

REMBMER: If you don't stand for something, you'll fall for anything.

FIRE

Chemists have divided fire into three parts - calorific rays, actinic rays and luminous energy. We recognize heat and light (calorific rays and luminous energy) and the actinic rays are that which creates change, turning wood into ashes, iron into steel, sand into glass.

In the Bible, fire has always been used as the symbol of deity. There was the flaming sword in the Garden of Eden, the burning bush which Moses saw in the desert, fire on Elijah's altar, and tongues of fire as the Holy Spirit fell on believers on the Day of Pentecost.

The **warmth** of God's fire draws all of us to Him as those who have long been out in the cold, suffering and chilled. We are drawn to Him for life and health as sunbathers expose themselves to the rays of the sun for health and strength. Here we find comfort and restoration for our weather-beaten souls after being exposed to the elements of bitterness, accusation and frustration.

Light, too, is found in God's fire for Jesus is the Light of the World and He sends us as lights into the world to carry His truth and life. It is this light that brings about growth in hearts and lives as the warmth of the sun brings about growth in the plant and animal world.

God's fire is **transforming** as well for we are never the same once we have felt His fire in our souls. We become new creations in Christ Jesus and slowly begin to take on His likeness. How miraculous the change that comes into the life of a believer! The glow shows on the face of one who's been with Him (Ex. 34:29).

REMEMBER: Fire burns away the dross from gold, and destroys the stubble that clutters our lives.

FOLLOW

Here is a word that is used several hundred times in Scripture. That alone makes it important. The meaning is not difficult, but putting it into practice can often consume a lifetime for Jesus said, "Come, follow me" and we never finish obeying that command of our Lord.

He associated several things with "following" Him. For instance, everyone who follows Jesus is to **deny himself** first. The things we have planned and the goals we have set for ourselves may have to be thrown out. They only weigh us down in pursuit of following Jesus. And we are to **"take up our cross"** as we follow Him. No prospect is too bleak, no burden too heavy to accept as we seek to pattern our lives after His.

Contrary to what we would expect, carrying a cross helps us in following Jesus rather than hindering us. Paul taught us to "follow after the things which make for peace" (Rom. 14:19). The pursuit of wealth, fame, pleasure or power does *anything* but make for peace because in seeking these things, we so often antagonize, brutalize and utilize other people to their detriment, leaving behind a trail of broken, hostile enemies in our wake.

How different to follow Christ and to exalt Him! Paul boldly taught that believers should follow Him as he followed Christ. Paul set himself up as an example of the kind of Christian life that others should imitate. He must have done some soul searching before he said such a thing! How wonderful if each of us as believers had the confidence in our own walk with the Lord to say the same thing!

REMEMBER: May God help us to follow Him, lead others to Him and never get in the way of His work among us on this earth.

FRUSTRATE

This word is part and parcel of modern life. On every hand, we find it more and more difficult to do the things we want to do - we're foiled in our attempts at many things. Our lack of success in reaching our goals may be due to immaturity and maladjustment, but the result is a complex, fitful situation that makes us unhappy and hostile (Gal. 3:21).

The Lord is a frustrator for He keeps the projections of liars from coming true, He drives fortunetellers crazy, and those who are wise in their own eyes, He brings to foolishness. Isaiah comforted the righteous when he promised that God would frustrate the designs of the wicked. When Ezra was rebuilding the temple in the land of Israel (Ezra 4:5), his enemies hired "counselors ... to frustrate" the work God had given Ezra to do. When we refuse to believe in Jesus, we frustrate the grace of God, making the death of Christ ineffective in our lives. By faith, however, we can stop frustrating the grace of God. By remaining faithful to God's work, we can refuse to let His work be frustrated by our enemies. When we look to God for our strength and ability to "keep on keeping on", we don't have to be frustrated in doing God's will.

Worry is a lack of faith in God and His power to bring about His final outcome of all things. Worry frustrates us into complete inactivity and apprehension. How unnecessary it is to be frustrated by worry - or anything else! God is in control of all things and who can foil, frustrate or prevent God from doing anything He decides to do? He is all powerful, and no one can keep Him from doing the things He has planned to do. Nothing can frustrate God's plans for us.

REMEMBER: God said, "I know the plans I have for you ... to give you a future and a hope" (Jer. 29:11 LB).

GAIUS

One of Paul's companions was a Greek from Macedonia called Gaius. He is mentioned several times in the New Testament. When Paul was in Ephesus, he was being persecuted. Even so, Gaius believed the Gospel Paul preached and accepted the possibility of suffering with God's people.

Gaius provided a place for Paul to stay just as so many others did when he was travelling from city to city throughout Asia Minor. Gaius was "given to hospitality" which tells you a lot about this man. Later, he became Paul's letter writer - perhaps a humble position for one who had previously been in the position of host. This host had a "host" of friends because he gave generously of all that he had (Rom. 16:23).

Sarah Coleman tells this story: "One young couple I knew had a great desire to witness for Jesus Christ and they didn't know quite how to go about it. They responded to the suggestion that they serve as hosts for a Bible study in their home and they hosted young people looking for a place to gather, missionaries who needed a haven for a while, others who needed a place to get away from the pressures of their lives. This couple became **hosts** for Jesus' sake. They were thrilled to know that Paul had commended Gaius for being his host!

"What a great idea and example for us all. If we have a home to share, we can share it 'in the name of Jesus' and make it more than just a gathering place. We can make it a praise to honor the name of our Savior. Gaius didn't exactly become famous for being a host and most of us don't know much about him today; still, Paul indicated that Gaius served human beings in a heavenly way."

REMEMBER: "Be not forgetful to entertain strangers; for some have entertained angels unawares" (Heb. 13:2).

GALATIANS

The churches in this area were built by Paul because he got sick and had to remain there longer than he had planned. The people in Galatia were country people and somewhat scattered. Being unsophisticated, they were confused when other teachers followed Paul telling them that they had to do good works to make their faith effective. Their arguments sounded plausible, and Paul's apostleship was discounted for he was not one of the twelve apostles who lived with Jesus before His death on the cross. These false teachers continued to add more and more rituals and responsibilities on the people - adding works to their faith for salvation. Paul wrote them the letter we call "Galatians" to remind them that salvation is by faith in Christ and nothing we can do will add to that. Salvation is by faith alone.

The Jews were accustomed to a system of sacrifices in which they placed their faith for cleansing from sin. They had forgotten that the lambs which they sacrificed only looked forward to the Lamb of God who was to come. When Jesus claimed to be that Lamb whom God had sent, they refused him and continued on in their animal sacrifices and temple worship. Paul wrote to the Galatians to free them of this system of blood sacrifices and rituals.

What must we do to be saved? We all seem to want to know. The answer is almost too simple to accept. Paul said, *"Believe on the Lord Jesus Christ and you will be saved"* (Acts 16:31). Jesus wasn't a trailblazer; He didn't come merely to set us a good example. Jesus came to be our Savior. We are to place our trust in Christ as the sacrifice for our sins. Our good works are done out of love for the fact that He has already saved us!

REMEMBER: Dead men cannot help themselves, and we were dead in sin. Only God could give us life.

GETHSEMANE

The old olive trees still stand - probably the same ones that were there in Jesus' day. They are gnarled and scarred, but alive. The grove lies near the bottom of a steep gorge outside the city of Jerusalem. It was beneath those olive trees that Jesus knelt and prayed, agonizing over your sin and mine (Mark 14:32-38).

To release the olive oil from the olives, they were placed on a flat stone across which another stone could grind the olives. A long pole was attached in such a way that weights were added on the end. For the first pressing of the olives, only one stone was hung on the end of the pole and the oil that came forth was pure and clear. Then, subsequent pressings were done with additional weight each time. As the weight increased, the pits and skins of the olives were crushed and filtered into the oil, leaving it less clear and pure. Gethsemane (the name, means "oil press") was where the pressure on Jesus began as He sweat great drops of blood and prayed desperately to His Father. Yet, His conclusion was, "Not My will, but Thine be done."

We know nothing like the suffering of Jesus as He knelt in that garden to pray, but we do experience suffering. God tells us to expect it. He also tells us that He is teaching us obedience when we suffer, but if we are to accept the suffering in our lives as from God and if we are to learn from it what God wants us to learn, we must pray as Jesus did. If He could not handle the suffering placed on Him without prayer, then surely we can't expect to handle ours without praying to our Heavenly Father until we, like Jesus, can say, *"Not my will, but Thine be done."* The writer of Hebrews tells us that even though Jesus was God's Son, He learned obedience through the things that He suffered.

REMEMBER: Let us pray that God will make our suffering effective to teach us to obey His will.

GIDEON

More than a thousand years before Christ, God spoke to Gideon and called him "a man of valor" (Judges 6:12). Gideon must have had a wry smile on his face for he (along with everyone else) knew that he was timid - a weakling. Many years later, Paul wrote that "God has chosen the weak things of this world to confound the wise", but at that moment in Gideon's life, he thought someone was making fun of him. The only thing Gideon had going for him was that he had faith in God even in those days of oppression by their enemies ..., even while his family members worshipped other gods.

Gideon had grown some wheat and when it came time to build his threshing floor, he built it in a gully instead of at the top of a hill as it was supposed to be built. He would need the breeze to blow away the chaff, and there wouldn't be much breeze down in that gully. Gideon had a reason, however, and that was his fear that their enemies would see him threshing and come to take his crop. So he was hiding in that gully when the angel found him and called him "a mighty man of valor". Hardly!

His assignment was to rescue Israel from their enemies, but Gideon needed more than a vision to know that God had really assigned him this challenge. Gideon believed God could save them from their enemies, but he wanted to be sure that he wasn't imagining things. He had no desire to stick his neck out and have it chopped off. So he asked for a sign and God gave it to him. Then, Gideon asked for another sign, and God gave him another. Finally convinced that it was truly God who had spoken, Gideon did as he was commanded and led the Israelites against their foes. Their victory is a matter of record.

REMEMBER: God and you are a majority and there is nothing that God wants to do that He won't do.

GIVE

When people hear this word in church, there is a universal move to protect their wallets, and one of the big complaints about preachers is that they are always asking for money. Actually, however, giving is spoken of over and over again in God's Word - quite often to remind us of all that we have received. It is also used many times to tell us of God's greatest gift to us, the Lord Jesus Christ and His death on the cross in our place.

"The wages of sin is death, but **the gift of God** is eternal life through Jesus Christ our Lord" (Rom 6:23).

The giving of a gift is to turn over possession or control without cost or exchange, and we receive eternal life without cost to ourselves. Through Jesus, we freely receive eternal life instead of the death we deserve beacuse of our sin.

If we are adamant that we are not sinners, then we will not reach out and take the gift of eternal life. God isn't trying to make us grovel before Him when He requires that we acknowledge our sin. It's just that we have no need of His gift unless we admit that we are sinners and in need of eternal life. When we confess our sinfulness, then we want His gift and He willingly gives it to us.

When we accept a magnificent gift from a friend, we are bound to him in love and the gift he has given is a bond of love between friends. A diamond ring signifies the close ties that make someone desirous of giving a valuable gift. God's gift cost Him the life of His Son, so when we accept the gift of eternal life, we are accepting an extremely valuable gift - it cost a lot! Such a gift binds us to the Giver in love and happiness.

REMEMBER: We love God because He first loved us ... and sent His Son to die for our sins.

GLAD

Some people just seem to be born happy, and David, the psalmist, was one of those people. He wrote psalms (songs) and many of them tell of his joy and pleasure in thinking about God and all that He has done.

"I have set the Lord always before me; because He is at my right hand, I shall not be moved. Therefore my heart is glad, and my glory rejoices; my flesh also shall rest in hope" (Ps. 16:8,9).

David put God first and it made him happy. In Psalm 100, David tells us to serve the Lord with gladness - which tells us that it is possible to serve the Lord without gladness! Still, when we remember that He is God, that He has made us and that we are His sheep, we can be glad and serve Him with singing as David did. David reminds us that "the Lord is good; His mercy is everlasting; and His truth endures to all generations." That is more than enough to make us glad!

An old sheepherder had a violin he loved to play, but he had no way of getting it in tune. So, he wrote to a local radio station and asked that they play an "A" at a given time so that he could tune his violin properly. They complied with his request and again, his instrument filled the air with glad music. If you aren't experiencing the joy of the Lord, perhaps you haven't taken time to get yourself in tune with God and you are left with discouragement and a feeling of being out of tune with everything and everyone. Set your life by God's pure tone and you will find that everything else falls into place. When we live our lives by faith in Jesus Christ, the music we live by is glad. Faith in Christ produces a glad heart, overflowing with joy.

REMEMBER: The Psalmist said, "I will sing unto the Lord, for He has made me glad."

GLORY

A baby boy was born in Israel at the time the Ark of the Covenant was captured by their enemies. This humiliating defeat was carried over into the name given him by his parents. They called him Ichabod which means "inglorious". The glory of Israel was in the hands of their enemies. Their glory (the presence of God) had left them and they had no other glory to claim (I Sam. 4:21).

In contrast, a man like Abraham who had wealth and position was called a "kabod", the opposite of "ichabod". Abraham's glory was demonstrated in his possessions and in the way he was clothed in fine linen. His flocks and his servants also commanded respect for he had large flocks and his servants were many. No wonder this is translated into the idea of honor and glory for God. The Hebrew "kabod" becomes "doxa" in Greek and we get our Doxology from that root. When we sing the Doxology, we sing praise and give glory to God.

Solomon was a king of great glory. He had unimaginable wealth and the splendor of his court was famous in his day. Other kings and queens came just to get a glimpse of Solomon's glory. Yet Jesus said that God is so lavish that He clothes the lilies of the field more gloriously than Solomon even though they last only a day.

In Revelation, we are astounded by the glory that this simple carpenter from Nazareth will have when He comes again. John fell at His feet "as dead" when he saw Him. His glory is beyond anything we can imagine, and "when we see Him, we shall be like Him," we are told.

REMEMBER: "To God be the glory, Great things He has done."

GO

This little word is used more than 1,300 times from Genesis to Revelation and it is part of the words "God", "Gospel" and "good". We find this little word used in the most important passages, such as, "Go ye into all the world and preach the Gospel to every creature" (Mk. 16:15), and "Go ... tell ... what great things the Lord has done for thee" (Mk. 5:19).

An old man named Luigi Tarisio was found dead one morning in his home. His house was sparsely furnished and reflected poverty, yet in his attic, he had 246 valuable violins! The oldest was a 147-year-old Stradavarius. Obviously, Luigi treasured these violins, but by hoarding them in his attic, he deprived the world of the glorious music they could produce. Some of us Christians are like that! We treasure the Gospel story and the riches we have in Christ, but instead of displaying them for all to see, we hoard them away in our spiritual attics and never bring them out into the light. It was for this reason that Christ said that we are to be like a city set on a hill where everyone for miles around can see that we belong to God. We are to be a light which is NOT hidden under a bushel basket but set up on a candlestick to give light to all those around.

It is not enough to know Christ - we are also to make Him known to everyone we can reach and who will hear what we have to say. We've been redeemd by the blood of Jesus which is more precious than gold and jewels - can we refuse to let others know about this marvel? Certainly not! When Jesus healed the man from Gadara, He sent him away to "tell what great things the Lord has done for thee". That is His command to us. Has Jesus lifted you out of sin? Tell your friends! Has he made your life worth living? Tell the world!

REMEMBER: There is a compelling GO in the Gospel!

GOD

A definition of God presents us with a huge task. The Bible does not define Him, but assumes His presence in our world and His power in creating and maintaining it. God says that He is who He is and we are left to learn who He is by what He does and what He tells us.

We hear from Genesis that God created the heavens and the earth, so He must be outside of them - bigger than they are - to have created the galaxies and put them in space. We understand that He must have existed before He created the world and everything in it, so we conclude that He had life in eternity past. He tells us that he "always was" and we are given to believe that He is eternal. He claims to have power over all the world and everything in it, so we are taught that He is all-powerful and no one can stand against Him. The Psalmist wrote that whether in the highest heaven or the lowest hell, God was there, so we conclude that He is infinite.

This is the way we define God - by what we know of Him and what He told us of Himself. Jesus told us that God is a spirit and that we are to worship Him in spirit and in truth. He also told us that God loved the world so much that He gave His only Son to die for our sins, and Paul wrote that He is the same yesterday, today and forever.

In spite of the Bible truths about God, many of us put someone or something into His place in our lives. Instead of giving Him the honor due His name, we exalt a spouse or a friend, a house or an automobile above all else in our lives. Give the deepest adoration and praise of your heart to God ALONE!

REMEMBER: Get your definition for God from the Book dedicated to telling us who He is - the Bible.

GOLGOTHA

There is a rooftop built next to the north wall of the city of Jerusalem from which you can see the hill called, "The Skull" (Luke 15:22). As evening fell, we stood looking down at this knoll and we could see the caves which form the "eyes" and "nose"of the skull. Off to the left, we saw the treetops of the grove which grows in the Garden of the Tomb where another cave lies with the trough where the stone was rolled to cover the tomb. There are differing opinions about the exact location of Jesus' tomb, but it is not hard to see why this hill is called "the Skull" and how logical it would have been to bury Jesus nearby.

Jesus was arrested on the east side of the city - outside the gates, down in the Valley of Kidron, but He was returned to the city for trial. His Disciples fled in every direction in fear of their lives. Only Peter followed a long way off. The religious rulers kept him all night and Caiaphas ruled over those proceedings. He was a Jew and it was Jews who testified against Jesus. Their hatred seemed to know no bounds. In the morning, they took Jesus to the Romans since they were the conquerors who ruled the land of Israel in those days. The Jews had not been given permission to put anyone to death, so they had to take Him to the Romans for permission. The trouble was, Pilate found no fault in Him and wasn't willing to put Him to death!

Still,the Jews were so riled up that Pilate eventually caved in to their demands, so Jesus was led to Golgotha—the Place of the Skull. Jesus stood on the hill, Mount Moriah, where Abraham had offered his son, but God intervened and provided a ram. How significant that in Jesus' day, God offered His own Son as our sacrifice—and this time, no one intervened..

REMEMBER: Jesus died so that we can live. Don't let His sacrifice be for nothing.

GOSPEL

The Old Testament gives us a history of the Jews and tells us of the system of sacrifice by which they lived, but in the New Testament, we have "good news" - the Gospel of Jesus Christ. We only find this word in the New Testament and the most concise definition of the gospel is found in I Corinthians 15:1-3:

"Christ died according to the Scriptures, was buried and rose again the third day, according to the Scriptures."

The Gospel is the story of Jesus and what He did. Paul expanded his teaching to include everything concerning the church, her responsibilities and relationships. He explained who was to carry certain responsibilities and what their lives were to be like, but nothing was to contradict the truth of Jesus' death, burial and resurrection.

Paul spoke to all (even rulers) with authority and urgency, trying to move them to accept the Gospel and live by it. His courage knew no bounds. Any so-called "gospel" that denied the deity of Jesus Christ was called "another gospel" which was not truly a gospel at all, but a misleading lie whose teachers were to be rejected. Napoleon wrote, "I search in vain in history to find anyone similar to Jesus Christ, or anything which can approach the gospel. Neither history, nor humanity, nor the ages, nor nature offer me anything with which I am able to compare or explain it. There is nothing there which is not beyond human mind. What happiness it gives to those who believe it."

How right he was! the story of Jeus is unlike any other and has no parallel in history. Believers find great joy in it.

REMEMBER: "Today is the day of salvation." "If you will believe, harden not your heart."

GOVERNMENT

Often we think of government as being separate from things that are spiritual; however, government is mentioned several times in the Bible and there is a great deal of teaching about government found there. This should not surprise us since all power belongs to God and those who have authority have it because God has placed that responsibility on their shoulders. Many who govern, however, seem to be unaware that they are going to have to answer to God for the way in which they use that authority to govern since their "power" has come from Him.

Jesus made this clear when He told Pilate that he would have no authority over Him *"unless it had been given to you from above"* even when Pilate threatened to put him to death. Concerning Jesus, Isaiah 9:6 says that *"the government shall be upon His shoulder"* and His title, *"King of kings"*, pointedly places Jesus as the greatest governor of time and eternity. Jesus said, *"All power is given to Me both in heaven and in earth"* and of His *"kingdom there will be no end"* (Matt. 25:8, Luke 11:33).

When Moses was overworked with the responsibilities of his leadership of the Children of Israel, God gave him a plan to divide the people into groups and put an able man in charge of each one. These leaders were to be men who feared God, were truthful and hated greed. Some ruled thousands of people, some ruled hundreds, some fifties and some ruled ten people. This responsibility to govern was given them from God, through Moses - each layer of government held responsible to govern in the realization that they were answerable to a higher power. Thus, in the home, in the church and in the nations, we are to be guided and controlled by those whom God has set in authority to govern that area of our lives.

REMEMBER: "The powers that be are ordained of God."

GRACE

This word has many meanings and many uses in the English language. It can mean "an exemption from penalty" as a grace period when your insurance policy is still in force even if the payment is late. It can refer to being in favor with someone as "in their good graces". Grace is used for the blessing asked of God before a meal when someone says grace. It is also used in "graceful", "gracious" and many other words which describe a pleasing quality. In Scripture, more than forty books of the Bible contain this word for it is most often and most fully used in connection with God. God is gracious and has shown His grace through Jesus Christ for no one could require Him to die for us, but He chose to give Himself out of His love for us. That's grace!

> *"For by grace are you saved, through faith and that not of yourselves, it is the gift of God"* (Eph. 2:8).

As believers, we also live by grace for when Paul suffered and found no relief, God said to him, *"My grace is sufficient for you"*. We often say, "I can't stand it! I can't take any more", but God says to us that we CAN take it. If we will call upon His power, He will give us the grace we need to accept the trials of life which so often wear on and on, seemingly without resolution for God sometimes gives us the grace to live with them and still find His joy. Paul also said,

> *"I am what I am by the grace of God, and His grace bestowed upon me was not in vain, and I labored more than them all, yet not I, but the grace of God which was with me"* (I Cor. 15:10).

REMEMBER: Who we are and what we do are not our own doing—these things are accomplished by God's grace so that He may have all the glory.

GUARD

The Bible uses both the word "guard" and the word "keep" to describe the way God takes care of His children. Peter wrote that we are *"**kept** by His power through faith unto salvation"*. We are told by Paul that *"the peace of God will **keep** your hearts and minds through Christ Jesus"* (Phil. 4:6,7).

In Jesus' day, the Roman Empire was the greatest power on earth and they had many prisons for those who fell into disfavor. Because of his preaching, and the fact that people were hostile to what he had to say, Paul was thrown into prison as a troublemaker. In Acts 16, we read the story of the guard whose responsibility it was to see that Paul stayed in prison. Paul and Silas prayed while they were locked up in that dismal prison, and they sang songs because they felt honored *"to suffer for Jesus' sake"*. An earthquake shook the prison that night and the guard thought his prisoners had escaped. Resigned to his fate, he drew his sword to take his own life for he knew that was the price for losing his prisoners, but Paul called out to tell him that they were all still there. The guard suddenly realized that Paul was free and he, himself, was the one who was bound by sin. He asked what he had to do to be saved from the chains of sin that bound his heart and soul. Paul gladly told him to believe on the Lord Jesus Christ and he would be saved. That same night, the guard took Paul and Silas into his house, prepared a meal for them and they all rejoiced in the freedom of sins forgiven. The guard from the prison had found a Savior to guard him and guide him the rest of his days. So it is that God will guard those of us who trust in Him. He gives His angels the responsibility of guarding us *"in all our ways"* says Psalm 91.

REMEMBER: "He that has begun a good work in you will perform it until the day of Jesus Christ" (Phil 1:6).

GUIDE

When travelling through new territory, we all need a guide—someone who knows the area and can direct us successfully through the unknown. Our lives are new territory—the future is uncharted and unknown. Each day, as we enter the unknown, we need a guide who knows the area and can take us through successfully. But who knows the future? Only God. Isn't it wonderful, then, that He offers to show us the way?

"I will instruct thee and teach thee in the way which thou shalt go; I will guide thee with mine eye" (Ps. 32:8).

Paul told the Christians at Colosse that *"the peace of Christ"* was to rule in their hearts - if they had peace in their hearts concerning a matter, it was good. If they didn't have peace about something, they were to seek another answer - another way to handle the problem. God's peace would be like an umpire to call the decisions of their lives.

Of course, many things God has taught us are clear and are to be accepted at face value, but where we are dealing with specific situations where there is no clear-cut teaching, God's peace will tell us when we are doing the things that please Him. The Psalmist wrote,

"This is God, our God forever and ever; He will be our guide, even unto death" (Ps. 48:14).

He also said, *"He knows the way I take"*. This Guide knows how to lead us successfully through life. Much of His guidance is given to us in His Word, but beyond that He leads us by the peace which He gives or withholds in our hearts.

REMEMBER: "Thou wilt keep him in perfect peace whose mind is stayed on Thee because he trusts in Thee" (Isa. 26:3).

HALLELUJAH

This word is the same in every language and it means "praise Jehovah". The eye can recognize that "jah" at the end refers to "Jehovah". George F. Handel immortalized this word in the majestic, "Hallelujah Chorus". Although this glorious chorus has few other words, they tell us why we are to praise God - *"for the Lord God omnipotent reigneth forever and ever. Amen."* God is in control and for that we are to be eternally grateful and glad.

Henry Bosch in "Our Daily Bread" wrote of one family which was suffering during the Depression because the father, a baker, had been injured and could not work. Mary Kimbrough's mother decided that since their flour bin was empty, they should take that moment to praise God. She called her family together and asked them all to say "Hallelujah". They all joined in the time of praise. Within a few minutes, they were the grateful recipients of bread, buns and cookies from the bakery where her husband usually worked. They were overbaked - too brown to sell, but not burned. "They tasted delicious to our family who had fully trusted God for our daily bread," recounted Mary.

Life has its empty moments - times that are bleak and dark, leaving us feeling helpless and hopeless. Betrayal, desertion, disease, injury - many things can stain our lives and make it seem foolish to praise God, but if we can praise Him in those moments, by faith, we will find strength and joy returning to our wounded souls. God will honor the faith with which we praise Him in spite of our circumstances.

How much better it is to praise God even in desperate straits than to murmur and complain - only making matters worse!

REMEMBER: We are to "offer the sacrifice of praise to God ... giving thanks to His name" for He gave Himself for us.

HEAVEN

Heaven is a real place for real people, but for many of us, it is the things that will NOT be there that lend the most appeal to heaven. In heaven, there will be no more death and no more crying which indicates that there will be nothing there to make us sad or distressed - no anxiety, no ulcers, no grief, no suffering. Specifically, the Bible tells us that *"there will be no more pain"* (Rev. 21:4). Most of us can say "Hallelujah" for that! There will be no night there, either, for Jesus ("the Light of the World") is also the Light of Heaven—His glory will create more light than we could bear had we not already received our heavenly bodies.

When Adam and Eve sinned, God placed a curse upon the earth and said that man would earn his living *"by the sweat of his brow"* and that women would bear children in pain. These effects of sin will be removed and there will be no more curse on the earth - no weeds, no insects, no wind and hail to knock down the crops the farmer labored so hard to cultivate, no rain to cause the grain to rot in the field. The curse of sin will be removed and productivity will be unimpaired.

Heaven will also contain some unusual things. We worship God here and sometimes feel His presence with us in a marvelous way, but in heaven we will have unbroken fellowship with Him—no limit on time or understanding, only His full attention and blessings. We will enjoy His *"pleasures forevermore"*. Now we can only know Him within the context of our human minds, but then we will see Him face to face and share His love and goodness with "no holds barred". Now, we believe in Him and serve Him even though we have not yet seen Him, but in heaven, we will serve Him and experience the joy of pleasing Him.

REMEMBER: We're not only saved from going to Hell, we are saved in order to go to Heaven.

HEAVENS

Today, scientists are talking a great deal about the "Big Bang" theory of creation and their ideas are coming closer to the story of beginnings as told to us in the Bible. But not only did earth and heaven begin with a "Big Bang", they will also end with a big bang. Second Peter 3:10 says that the heavens' *"will pass away with a great noise, and the elements shall melt with fervent heat."* In Revelation, the Apostle John tells us that there will someday be *"a new heaven and a new earth, for the first heaven and the first earth"* will pass away. After that, John goes on to describe the Heavenly City where everything is new *"for the former things have passed away"*.

The light of this city is unlike anything we have ever seen for it is clear as crystal - no smog in Heaven! The city is square and has twelve gates, each with an angel standing by, and each has one of the names of the twelve tribes of the Children of Israel. The wall is great and as high as each side of the city is long. The length and height and width are all equal. It has twelve foundations with the names of the Apostles on them. The wall is made of precious stone so perfect it is clear. The city is made of gold so pure that it is clear like glass. Precious stones are everywhere and they are larger than any precious stones we have ever imagined.

There is no church in this city - for the Lamb of God Himself is the temple there. The gates never shut and kings shall come so that their glory is lost in the greater glory of God. *"They shall bring the glory and honor of the nations into it."* Moreover, there will be nothing in that city to defile it and the people there will be those whose names are written in the Lamb's Book of Life.

REMEMBER: If your name is written there, it is because you have believed in Jesus, the spotless Lamb of God.

HEZEKIAH

This young man became the king of Israel when he was twenty-five years old, but even at that early age, he already loved God and wanted to please Him. His first project was to open the temple and repair the doors so his people could once again worship there. Then he brought back the priests and the Levites to cleanse the temple and to restore the sacrifices. He reigned for twenty-nine years and the people prospered under his leadership.

An enemy (King Sennacherib) marched against Jerusalem and Hezekiah decided to stop up all the springs so that the King would not desire so dry and arid a land. Then he encouraged his people in the face of this mighty enemy for Hezekiah said, *"With us is the Lord our God, to help us and to fight our battles."* When the King came, he told Hezekiah's people that the gods of the other nations had not kept him from capturing them, so their God would not be able to deliver them, either. He mocked Hezekiah and told the people not to trust him. He even wrote a letter to Hezekiah asking where the other kings were whom Sennacherib had destroyed.

This godly king took the letter to the Lord's house and spread it out before God. Hezekiah prayed that God would deliver them so that *"all the kingdoms of the earth may know that You are the Lord God, You alone."* God heard his prayer and God said, *"He shall not come into this city ... by the way that he came, By the same shall he return. I will defend this city, save it for My own sake."* Then, one night the angel of the Lord went into the camp of the enemy and killed 185,000 men. When the rest woke up in the morning, they were surrounded by corpses. Their king went home and was killed by two of his own sons.

REMEMBER: "More things are wrought by prayer than this world dreams of."

HOPE

Two women stood watching a funeral procession. One asked the other what was going on. "This is the burying of a missionary's son," she said. "How sad!" the other replied. "It isn't as bad for them as it is for us when we bury our sons," she spoke thoughtfully. "They know something that makes them know they will get them back someday. We don't know how to get our sons back. With us, it is hopeless!"

It's true! *"We sorrow not as those who have no hope"* for we know that God will gather His children to spend eternity with Him. Yes, we sorrow when death takes our loved ones, but we have the wonderful hope of seeing them again. The separation is temporary - it is not forever. We have a *"sure and steadfast hope"* which is grounded in our Savior because He rose from the dead and He is only the first to do so. We, too, will be raised in newness of life to experience eternity together in His presence.

God is so dependable that Paul calls Him *"the God of hope"* and since Christ is in us, we have *"the hope of glory"*. We have hope that Jesus will come again and we will see Him.

> *"Whatever things were written before were written for our learning, that we through the patience and comfort of the Scriptures might have hope" (Rom. 15:4).*

How clearly this verse tells us that we find hope by reading the Bible! Life becomes very draining at times and we need the Scriptures in order to renew our hope in God. Don't wade through the mud of discouragement. Read God's Word and find hope! Hope in God never disappoints us.

REMEMBER: "Christ is risen from the dead, and has become the first ... among many brethren" to be raised in newness of life.

HOSEA

This name means "salvation" and was given to a Hebrew prophet in the eighth century B.C. He preached to the kings of Israel even though he was the son of a middle-class merchant. He had been educated well as were most boys in those days, but he also showed deep spiritual insight and a good mind. He saw the wayward practices of his countrymen and their carelessness in the worship of God. They had been commanded to be separate from the wicked nations that surrounded them; however, they had instead given themselves over to worship the gods of their neighbors. It was a system given over to drunkenness and immorality, full of magic, mythology and occultic practices. This was nothing like the purity and devotion that God required of His followers.

Hosea pointed this out and called the Children of Israel back to worship the true God. He reminded them that at Mount Sinai they pledged to worship and serve God alone. In the book that bears his name, Hosea used his own marriage as an illustration of Israel, the Bride of God. Hosea married a woman who bore his children, then proved to be unfaithful to him. After she was pursued by her lovers and had sinned, she was brought back to Hosea in disgrace. However, he loved her and patiently restored her to full favor in his home and in his heart. This was the picture for Israel had been joined to God in a special relationship, then went off to worship other gods. In disgrace, Israel returned to God, penitent and broken, and God in His great love restored her to the special place she had held. Undeserving, she was forgiven and blessed instead of suffering the consequences of sin.

REMEMBER: God calls us to return to Him even when we have shamed His name and sinned against Him. It only takes our confession of sin and "He is faithful and just to forgive us".

HUMILITY

Pride is one of the things God hates - in fact, it is the first thing on His list. We are told over and over that we are not to be proud, and if we are not proud, then we are humble.

"Be clothed with humility; for God resisteth the proud, and giveth grace to the humble" (I Peter 5:5).

Humility does not come naturally to the human heart and so we must put it on as we dress ourselves in our clothing every morning. We still strive to serve God in the best way we can but we adopt the attitude of a saint of bygone days, "Grant, oh Lord, that I may pass unnoticed through this world and yet bring glory to Thy name." Clearly, however, this perspective of life is rare, indeed.

One proud woman was mistakenly seated on the left of her British host rather than on the right which is the place of honor. She was offended and commented that the aide seemed unable to seat the guests at the table properly. The British official replied, "No, it is not a problem for I have found that those who matter, don't mind, and those who mind, don't matter!"

Even the disciples who walked with Jesus were caught arguing over who would have the best places on His right hand and on His left. Jesus emphasized to them that He had come to serve others and that, if they wanted to be great in His kingdom, they should be the servant of all. If they wanted to be first, they should be a slave to others. Jesus said that among His followers, things would be different than they are in other groups. In the service of Jesus Christ, the glory belongs to Him!

REMEMBER: "The Lord lifts up the humble; He casts the wicked down to the ground" (Ps. 147:6).

HYMN

Singing is the hallmark of real faith in God. The church is a place of music and often it is loud - very loud. David wrote the songs which we call "the Psalms" and he speaks of trumpets and loud, clanging cymbals being used in worship and praise of God. Many other religions have no music or else it is in the form of chants and dirges which tend to depress rather than to uplift the soul.

Believers have been found singing songs of praise in prisons, dungeons, in captivity as well as at home, at school and at church. Why not? When you know you have a Savior who will care for you now and throughout eternity, there is good cause to sing!

• The Pilgrims put to sea from Plymouth, England, with songs on their lips and in them they found courage for the voyage and the rigors of a new land.

• Hugh Mackaye of Scotland was hanged while singing, "In Thee, O Lord, do I put my trust" and his faith was rewarded that day as his soul went directly to heaven to be with Jesus.

If you have a Bible, you have a hymnbook - or a **Him book,** as some say. You don't need vocal training to sing praise to God. You only need a thankful heart. If you've neglected to sing His praise, perhaps it's because you've been neglecting Him! Look again at your Savior; think about the power He exercises in your life. Remember that He is God and we can safely trust in Him. Then, start to list all those things He does for you every day— literally count your blessings. Write them down and review His goodness to you. You'll soon find your song again even if life has not been kind to you.

REMEMBER: If we look around us, we are dismayed; but if we look up, we see Jesus and it's easy to sing His praises.

HYPOCRITE

When children pretend, it is a sign of a healthy mind and an active imagination. When grown-ups pretend, it is usually not a good sign at all. To pretend to be righteous while knowing that our lives don't measure up, is the worst kind of pretending— it is hypocrisy. However, the most useless kind of pretending is to try to fool God.

Since God knows all things, there is no way that we can convince Him that we are something that we are not - even if we fool everyone around us. Some people even try to help people and appear to be very thoughtful and kind while covering their own sins which may be worse than those of the person they are trying to help. How cynical we must be to offer to help someone else when we need help ourselves! Jesus asked,

"Why call ye me Lord, Lord, and do not the things which I say?" (Luke 6:46).

He was describing hypocrites who talk a good line, but don't do the good they so loudly proclaim. It is clear that Jesus is not so much interested in our claims as He is in our actions. He told the story of two sons - the one agreed to do what his father asked but didn't carry it out. The other refused to do his father's bidding, but after thinking it over, he complied. *"Which one was obedient?"* Jesus asked (Luke 15:11).

The clear answer is that the son who actually did what his father commanded was the obedient son. Our words are useless to convince our Heavenly Father, too, unless we follow through and actually live the life He has set out for us to live. No wonder Jesus placed such importance on obedience !

REMEMBER; "Be ye doers of the word and not hearers only ... deceiving yourselves" (James 1:22).

IDLE

This word has many "sound alikes" such as "idol", "idyll", and "ideal". However, we're not going to discuss "idols" (images or objects of worship), nor "idylls" (descriptions of a simple country scene), nor "ideals" (the perfect model).

Our word today is what Solomon had in mind when he wrote,

"By much slothfulness the building decays, and through idleness of the hands the house droppeth through" (Eccl. 10:18).

Neglect allows things that should be cared for to deteriorate. However, idleness creates other problems along with it. Older generations used to say that "an idle mind is the devil's workshop", and Paul found that was true in his day.

"We hear that there are some which walk among you in disorderly manner, working not at all, but they are busybodies" (II Thess. 3:ll).

Even idle words are condemned by Jesus, for He said,

"Every idle word that man shall speak, they shall give account thereof in the day of judgment. For by the words of your mouth you shall be justified, and by your word you shall be condemned" (Matt. 12:36,37).

A visiting minister was asked to lead in prayer in Sunday School. One girl was so impressed, she blurted out, "Gosh! What a prayer!" It's easy to see that "gosh" and "prayer" sound incongruous in the same breath, yet we hear oaths and foul talk that go far beyond these "minced oaths" almost everywhere we go.

REMEMBER: We will be held accountable to God for the things we say.

IDOL

One of the "sound alike" words we referred to, is "idol". The people who lived in the land of Israel before the Children of Israel came were people of great idolatry. They had places of worship set up in the mountains and there they bowed before images made by their own hands. They also had household gods - gods for every phase of life to whom they prayed for help.

People always seem to need someone or something higher than themselves to look to in times of stress and trouble. However, wherever God's people went, He sent them with instructions to "put away" and "destroy" all the idols, and to turn to the true God. God blessed His people when they worshipped Him alone. The first of the Ten Commandments says,

"Thou shalt have no other gods before Me. Thou shalt not make any graven image, any likeness of that which is in heaven or on earth" (Ex. 20:3,4).

From the first to the last of Scripture, there are severe warnings against idols and worship of idols.

"Take heed to yourselves, that your heart be not deceived, and ye turn aside, and serve other gods" (Deut. 11:16). "I am the Lord ... my glory will I not give to another, neither praise to graven images" (Isa. 42:8). "Little children, keep yourself from idols" (I John 5:21).

Many of us would not think of bowing before a statue, yet we look to education, pleasure and wealth for our source of strength instead of turning to God. Things on which we place more value than is due them have become our idols.

REMEMBER: Only the Living God is worthy to reign on the thrones of our hearts and homes.

IMAGE

Unlike some of our words, this one has come into **more** use lately than it had in years gone by, for now we seem to be obsessed with the image we project to others instead of placing our chief value on the kind of person we actually are. No doubt, this has a great deal to do with the place that television has come to hold in our lives and in society.

Still, even though we use this word more today, perhaps we have lost something of its meaning for in Scripture it meant much more than the outward appearance. It went much deeper than that when God said, *"Let us make man in our own image."* It was used in the same sense that Paul used when he referred to Jesus Christ as the *"image and glory of God"* (I Cor. 11:7), *"Christ who is the image of God"* (II C or. 4:4), and *"the image of the invisible God"* (Col. 1:15). In Romans 8:29, Paul tells us that believers are *"predestinated to be conformed to the image of His Son"*.

The human race was marred by sin in the Garden of Eden when Adam sinned. The original image of God at the creation of man has been disfigured by sin, and we need to be molded once again into God's image - *"the image of His Son"*.

No one has ever seen God's face for we can't bear to look upon His glory, yet Jesus came to show us what God is like. We have no sure knowledge of what Jesus **looked** like, but we can be sure that **His heart was revealed** in everything He did. When we understand His life, we can see what God is like. By making Jesus the center and core of our lives, we can become like Him and then we will reflect the glory of God. How vital, then, that we constantly turn our thoughts to Him and read His Word.

REMEMBER: When Moses talked with God, his face shone, reflecting the glory of God. Let us live so close to God that our faces shine with His glory.

INIQUITY

Some may dare to speak of a "little, white lie", but no one ever tries to detract from the ugliness of "iniquity" - a wicked act, a very great injustice. This word conveys the character of sin, showing it to be a great offense to God which it surely is.

Babylon and her people were wicked in God's sight and God *"remembered her iniquities"*. Sin must be punished, paid for, to appease the righteousness of God. Judgment of sin is certain. *"Whoso sinneth, he shall die,"* God declared in Ezekiel 18:4.

No wonder, then, that those who believe in Christ and find refuge from this judgment in Him are eternally grateful. He *"forgives all our iniquities"* - how great should be our praise to Him for no one else could pay the price for us. Each of us would have to die for our own sins - we are sinful, but Christ was sinless and, thus, could die for our sins since He had none of His own.

Our bent toward waywardness and perversity leads each one of us down the wrong road, away from God. We can *"be sure your sin will find you out"*—we always do the wrong thing because we are *"born in sin"* since our parents back to Adam and Eve were sinners—sinners beget sinners. We all need a Savior and there is only one!

> *"All we like sheep have gone astray, we have turned every one in his own way, but the Lord has laid on Him the iniquity of us all" (Isa. 53:6).*

By His death, Christ paid the penalty for our sin, yet we must come to a place of personal acceptance for His death to be effective for us. He will forgive all our iniquities.

REMEMBER: Jesus said, "Behold, if any man hears my voice and opens the door, I will come to him" (Rev. 3:20).

INSPIRATION

Only twice in all of Scripture do we find this word:

"The inspiration of the Almighty gives understanding" (Job 32:8).

"All Scripture is given by inspiration of God" (II Tim. 3:16).

In spite of its scarcity, the truth it carries is of utmost importance because the understanding of our faith comes through the Scriptures - that is the means by which we learn how to live for our God.

"All Scripture is given by inspiration of God, and is profitable for doctrine, for reproof, for correction, for instruction in righteousness that the man of God may be perfect, thoroughly furnished unto all good works" (II Tim. 3:16).

The Old Testament is the history of God's dealings with His people, Israel, and in Jesus' day, that was all the Scripture they had. After Jesus lived and died, His story was written by those who walked the roads of Galilee with Him. He said,

"Heaven and earth will pass away, but My words shall not pass away" (Matt. 24:35).

Inspiration conveys the idea that all Scripture was breathed into the writers by God Himself. Scripture was not the creation of men, but God's creation put into writing by men - what a difference! The Bible is not a book contrived by the mind of man - it is God speaking through men - to people of all the ages.

REMEMBER: The Bible is not like any other book - it is God's love letter to each one who reads its pages.

INSTRUCTION

In Hebrew, the first five books of the Bible are called "Torah" - instruction. The word "torah", however, is not always capitalized; therefore, it is also used for "the word of the Lord" and has the wider sense of instruction from God. It can be used as a synonym for the revealed will of God, His commandments, His ways, His judgments and the precepts of the Lord. The Gospel, too, is considered to be instruction from the Lord for we are told that Scripture is profitable "for instruction in righteousness".

When we come to Christ for salvation, we often have little understanding of righteousness - what it is, how to achieve it, or even how important it is in the sight of God. However, it is in God's Word that we find our instructions on how to live the Christian life. Is it important to study theBible? It surely is! We are to learn from it as a son learns from a father who delights in him. Solomon was the wisest man that ever lived and he exhorts us to study and to learn:

"Hear, ye children, the instruction of a father, and attend to know understanding; For I was my father's son, tender and only beloved in the sight of my mother. He taught me also, and said unto me, Let thine heart retain my words; keep my commandments, and live. Get wisdom, get understanding; forget it not, neither decline from the words of my mouth. Forsake her not (wisdom), and she shall preserve thee; love her, and she shall keep thee. Wisdom is the principal thing; therefore, get wisdom; and with all thy getting, get understanding" (Prov. 4:1-7).

REMEMBER: Our Heavenly Father wants to instruct us in living righteously in this present world.

INSTRUMENT

Musical instruments are mentioned again and again in God's Word. No doubt, music is important to Him and He wants us to see that musicians who sing praises to God must be dedicated to Him - not divided between the music of the world and the heavenly music which brings honor to His name.

In Genesis, Jabal and Jubal were born to Adah. They were cattlemen and lived in tents, but Jubal invented the harp and the flute. So, from the earliest years of mankind, there were musical instruments and God gave the ability to make them and to make music with them.

The Bible's most famous musician was David. He is best known for his songs (the Psalms) but he was also a maker of instruments. He said that *"four thousand will praise the Lord with the musical instruments I have made"* (I Chron. 23), and in II Chronicles 7:6, we see that the priests were still using the instruments he had made and had used in praise to God.

David not only liked worship to be loud, as he points out many times in the Psalms, he also liked to have lots of music. He lists many instruments to be used in worship, and along with his songs, there can be no doubt of the place that music held for King David.

"Praise Him with the trumpet and with lute and harp. Praise Him with the tambourines and processional. Praise Him with stringed instruments and horns. Praise Him with the cymbals, yes, loud clanging cymbals. Let everything that has breath praise the Lord. Praise ye the Lord! Hallelujah!" (Ps. 150).

REMEMBER: Our very lives can be an instrument to bring praise to God. We can be an "instrument of God's peace".

INTERCESSION

This word refers to one person pleading for another, but especially it refers to one who prays to, pleads with, and believes in God on behalf of others. Prayer is our greatest power for "the eyes of the Lord are over the righteous, and His ears are open to their prayers" (I Peter 3:12). There is so much in life that we cannot change, we cannot do and we cannot control, but we can pray! There is nothing that God cannot change, nothing He cannot do, nothing He cannot or will not control in answer to our prayers

• Pray personally: God will hear even the smallest, most intimate words of prayer that we offer Him.

• Pray scripturally: He does not respond to our prayers on the basis of repetition. He already knows what we need. He's only waiting for us to ask Him, acknowledging our need and the fact that the answer will come from Him.

• Pray intelligently: Some people pray in generalities, but we can be much more effective when we pray specifically and directly about particular people and situations.

• Pray faithfully: Prayer is to be an integral part of our daily lives - not a crisis cop-out! God wants to respond to our daily needs, not just bail us out when the going gets tough.

• Pray intensely: Many times our hearts are heavy with concern and cares. These are the burdens that God places on our hearts to bring us to Him in prayer. Don't wade through the circumstances of life when God can lift you up and place your feet on a rock.

REMEMBER: Jesus' prayer was, "Not My will, but Thine be done." Our prayers will also bring us into line with God's will.

ISAIAH

The Old Testament prophet, Isaiah, was a prophet in Judah and heralded the coming of Jesus the Messiah 800 years before He came. Israel, the northern kingdom, had been destroyed by the Assyrians and Isaiah spoke loud and long to the people of the southern kingdom (Judah) about God and obedience to Him. He did not hesitate to speak of God's coming punishment for sin and he conveyed God's desire to *"reason together"* concerning their sins and His offer to cleanse them from sin- *"Though your sins be as scarlet, they shall be as white as snow."*

Isaiah presented the heart of the Old Testament in his prophecies:

• The person of Christ: He foretold the birth of Jesus in Bethlehem even though it was a small village - unheralded in any other way. Isaiah taught that Jesus' birth would be of a virgin contrary to all other births ever to occur. He gave us His name, Immanuel ("God with us"), for when Jesus came, it was God appearing in human flesh to show us God the Father.

• The suffering of Christ: In Isaiah 53, we have the detailed description of the death that Christ was to suffer. Crucifixion was gruesomely described even though this form of Roman cruelty had not yet been devised. Isaiah even said that we would think Jesus had been *"stricken by God"* and we would *"despise Him"*.

• The reign of Christ: Those many centuries ago, Isaiah knew that Christ's death would not be His end for He is yet to reign as King of kings and Lord of lords. Isaiah prophesied that Christ would bring good tidings to the meek, bind up the brokenhearted, set captives free, and reign on the earth.

REMEMBER: God's word will not fail, but will accomplish all that He plans to do in heaven and in earth.

JAMES

This name, still popular today, was also in popular use in Jesus' day. The Bible speaks of James, the son of Zebedee and a brother of the Apostle John. He was with Jesus and two other disciples on the Mount of Transfiguration and in the Garden of Gethsemane. He was among those who were very close to Jesus during His life on earth. Another of the disciples was named James and was called "James the Less" to distinguish between them. His father was Alphaeus.

Jesus had a half-brother who was called James, also - a son of Mary and Joseph. It was very hard for him to accept Jesus as the Messiah - he was too close to Him to see it until after the resurrection when he finally acknowledged that this one whom he knew so well was, indeed, the Messiah of God. However, when he came to this conviction, he became one of the leaders of the early church in Jerusalem. He presided at a church council in Jerusalem, we are told in Acts 15:21, and he became an advisor to the Apostle Paul later in his life. Jesus' brother was martyred by a Jewish high priest in 62 A.D. according to the great historian, Josephus. Finally, there was James who was the father of an apostle named Judas - not Judas Iscariot who betrayed Jesus.

James, the son of Zebedee, was martyred before the book of James was written, and many scholars believe it was Jesus' brother who wrote the book. He wrote with authority and his style is completely Jewish in its frame of reference. He demonstrates his great identification with the Law of Moses. The epistle bears a striking resemblance to the lofty morality and the grandeur of the Sermon on the Mount.

REMEMBER: As the brother of our Lord became "a servant of the Lord Jesus Christ", so we should serve Him, too.

JEHOVAH-NISSI

This name for God directs our attention to the fact that God is present with us - here and now! In Exodus 17, we read the story of a battle between the Children of Israel and the Amalekites, and God's people were losing! Only as Moses sat on a hill overlooking the battleground and raised his hands over his head in a plea to God for victory did His people prevail. When his arms tired, Aaron and Hur held them up so that the battle would be theirs. Since the enemy was stronger than they were, the Children of Israel knew that God had given them the victory - it was not by their own might.

In recognition of this, Moses built an altar which he called,"The Lord my banner". Not only the Children of Israel, but also the heathen nations around them recognized that God led the Israelites and gave them victories they could not have won for themselves. Melchizedek, king of Salem (Jerusalem), told Abraham that God had delivered his enemies into his hands ... the Lord was his banner!

David also used this name for God in Psalm 118 when he said, "The Lord is on my side; I will not fear what man can do unto me. It is better to trust in the Lord than to put confidence in man. All nations compassed me about: but in the name of the Lord I will destroy them!"

Jacob, too, found the presence of the Lord to be a reality. He had trouble at home, trouble on the road and trouble in that far country. Then one night, he wrestled with "a man" all night long and finally, the "man" gave him a new name - Israel - which means "you have power with God and man". Jacob said, "I have seen God face to face" - God was present with him.

REMEMBER: This was not a special privilege for Old Testament saints. God's desire is to be with each one of us.

JEHOVAH-SHALOM

Frequently, people say to one another, "Shalom", and Jews who keep the Sabbath say, "Shabbat shalom", but when we say "Jehovah-Shalom", we are saying that God is our peace.

After he saw the Angel of the Lord, Gideon built an altar and called it "Jehovah–Shalom" for the Lord had said to him, "Peace be unto you." Throughout His communications to people, God emphasizes and re-emphasizes His peace. At Jesus' birth, the angels offered God's peace to all mankind.

When Jesus left this earth, He spoke to His disciples telling them that He was leaving His peace with them and that it was not like earthly peace. After all, our peace is shattered at the first sign of trouble, but the peace that Jesus gives holds us firm and true in the midst of trouble because we know that the victory is ultimately in God's hands. Knowing God and thinking about Him is given throughout Scripture as the means by which we can have peace. It will "keep our hearts and minds through Christ Jesus".

- We have peace with God when we surrender our wills to His.

- We have peace from God in our lives even when our circumstances don't merit peace.

- We also have the peace of God to rule in our hearts for He IS our peace and He lives within each believer.

"In the world, you will have tribulation; but be of good cheer for I have overcome the world" (Jn. 16:33).

REMEMBER: There is no peace for the wicked, but those of us who believe in God are promised peace when we set our minds on Him.

JEHOVAH-TSIDKENU

We recognize Jehovah, of course, but what a strange word is "tsidkenu". Still, in spite of its strange sound, we all know about its meaning - the Lord our righteousness. Every human heart has a desire for the perfection and "rightness" of which this name speaks. We see our own failings and look for those things which are better and higher than anything we can achieve. Our waywardness overtakes us repeatedly, but God calls us to His righteousness.

The people of Israel were wayward, too, and time after time, they allowed their dedication to God to slip from their grasp as they became involved with the wicked nations that surrounded them. God punished them and called them to return to Him by allowing great armies to conquer their land and their people. Then in the days of suffering that followed, God would send His messenger to call them to repent and turn again to Him. When they did, He never failed to respond to their helpless cries with love and restoration. He was *"the Lord their righteousness"*.

We're very much like them, aren't we? We love God and we dedicate ourselves to Him, but then we get busy with our lives and responsibilities and allow the things of this world to crowd out our devotion to Him. He calls us back to His side - often by trials and tribulations in our lives. Yet, when we call upon Him for deliverance and help, He hears our cry and forgives us, cleanses us, and restores our fellowship with Him. It is with our hearts that we *"believe unto righteousness"* (Rom 10:10). He is *"the Lord **our** righteousness"*.

REMEMBER: God delights in pardoning our past and empowering our present. He gives new hearts for new beginnings.

JEREMIAH

A popular name for children these days is "Jeremy" which is from the same root as Jeremiah and means "Jehovah exalts". The Old Testament prophet by this name was born into a family of priests in a small town near Jerusalem. The book of the Bible that bears his name is auto-biographical and we can know a great deal about his life from reading it.

As a young man, Jeremiah felt God's call to him to preach, but he felt too young and immature and spoke to God of his reluctance to accept so much responsibility at such a young age. God reassured him, however, promising him divine strength and wisdom, so Jeremiah became a devoted servant of God.

His message of repentance was not welcomed by his countrymen in spite of the fact that Jeremiah spoke for God, and Jeremiah was persecuted for his devotion to God's truth. He wept over the sinful state of his nation. He told them the city of Jerusalem would be destroyed unless they repented. They didn't, and it was destroyed! When the Babylonians took the city, Jeremiah was to remain with the people there, but instead, they took him and fled to Egypt. That is probably where he died, but his sermons remain to this day.

One day, God sent him to the house of a potter to watch him as he worked. He sat at the wheel, making a clay pot, but it was imperfect and he smashed it and re-made it into another jar. God said that His people are as clay in His hand and He can make of them whatever He wills. He warned that He was "fashioning a disaster" for those who would not repent and return to Him.

REMEMBER: God, the potter, molds us to His plan, but He also invites us to call upon Him and He will "answer and show thee great and mighty things which thou knowest not" (Jer. 33:3).

JESUS

In Hebrew this name is Joshua, but in its Greek form, we know it best—Jesus. This name is in common use in many cultures. Part of Cambridge University is called Jesus College - it was founded in 1496. Not only has this name been in common use throughout the centuries, but, sadly, it has become a curse word to many. However, when we use it without further definition, we mean Jesus Christ of Nazareth who lived in the first century in the land of Israel.

Before Jesus was conceived in Mary's womb, His name was foretold to Joseph along with the prophecy of His life—"*He shall save His people from their sins*". This name was the last to be uttered by Charles Sprugeon as he delivered his last address in Exeter Hall in London. He longed to leave the name of Jesus as a legacy to all who followed.

Throughout the ages of time, there have been millions who have loved and cherished the name of Jesus because of His great love to us. Who else could save our souls and give us a place in heaven for eternity? No one! "Jesus! How sweet the name!" wrote the hymn writer.

The angels announced His birth, and they were present when He returned to heaven. They brought good news on each occasion, for they sang glory to God and peace on earth at His coming. When He ascended into heaven, they promised that *"this same Jesus, shall so come in like manner as ye have seen Him go"*. His coming again is a sure promise delivered to us by the angels of heaven.

REMEMBER: When He comes again, every eye will see Him and we will recognize Him as Lord and Savior. Why wait? Receive Him as your Lord and Savior today.

JOB

This man is said to have lived in the days of Genesis and this book was written before any of the other books. The Bible is not arranged in chronological order, but by subject; that is, the books of the law come first (five of them); history follows; then books of poetry of which Job is but one. Prophecy is the category for the remaining books of the Old Testament.

Job is beautifully written and presents a picture of the grandeur and majesty of God unparalleled anywhere. We also learn a lot about Job himself in this book. He was a man of good character, he honored God in his life, and he avoided anything wicked or evil. He had a family which brought him a great deal of happiness. Also, he was wealthy and well-known—*"greatest of all the children of the East"*, it is said.

He was so outstanding that an argument began in heaven concerning him, the devil saying it was no wonder Job loved God since he had everything a man could want! The devil challenged that Job would desert his faith if those things were taken from him. God allowed him to test Job by removing all the earthly blessings from him, but Job remained faithful to God even in the midst of physical suffering, loss of his wealth and his family. His wife told him t*o "curse God and die"!* His friends accused him of secret sin for they couldn't imagine anyone suffering so much without having done something terrible. In spite of his awful situation Job said, *"I know that my Redeemer lives, and He shall stand at the latter day upon the earth. Though worms destroy my body, yet in my flesh shall I see God."* Job held the promise of eternity with his Redeemer to be true no matter what life brought.

REMEMBER: We're told that "the Lord blessed the latter days of Job more than his beginning". He was restored on earth and will be resurrected at the last day as well!

JOEL

This name was fairly common among the Hebrews of Old Testament days and more than a dozen men by this name are mentioned there. It means "Jehovah is God" so we can readily see why it was so widely used. The book of the Bible by this name was written several hundred years before Christ. As with other prophets, his job was to point out Israel's sin and to call them to repentance.

His prophecy has a double meaning for it applied to the countrymen of his day as well as being a prediction of world events in the end times. Joel described a plague of locusts who came and ate everything in their path, leaving the people of the land in famine. Joel thundered against their sin, warning against *"the day of the Lord"* in which God's judgment would be poured out on them. He did not neglect to remind them, too, of God's promised blessings if they would obey and serve Him.

As Joel preached and prophesied, the people listened in indecision - they couldn't decide if this man was from God or just some "loony" who had been out in the hot sun too long. Their indecision lingered and they seemed unable to break the inertia that gripped them.

So many today hear the Word of God, but, like Israel of old, they too wonder just how seriously they should take the truth they hear. Is this really something they should use to re-design their lives? Perhaps those who witness of God are not to be taken so seriously! In their wondering, they delay making a decision as the time of judgment gets closer and closer.

REMEMBER: TODAY is the day of salvation. TODAY if you hear God's voice, come to Him while there is still time.

JOHN

The Apostle John loved Jesus and he loved people. He wrote one of the most intimate letters in the Bible, calling them "my little children" out of his heart of love and the many years of his life.

He had been a young man when Jesus walked the earth, yet he still lived and wrote around 90 A.D. Earlier, he had written of Jesus' life in the Gospel of John, but in his little letters, he speaks of sin as a child's offense against his father and teaches that it was to be cared for as a family matter. The world outside is viewed as an evil influence.

John wrote with warnings against pretending to be something we are not and claiming to be more than we are, but he goes on to say that when we are honest with God, He receives us and forgives us. John pleads with believers to *"hold fast to the faith"* as long as we live. Like an older brother, John assures us of eternal life which we have received from God and reassures us that God will hear and answer our prayers according to His will.

His second letter warns against false teachers and calls on us to hold fast to the commandments we have received from God. The third letter names people who have been hospitable ... and those who have not. At this point in his life, John has the seniority to be direct with his readers. As always, John isn't into "playing games" - he calls them to be honest with God and with each other. He had no duplicity in him and he challenged others to be open and honest, too. Pride, greed and selfishness are condemned publicly. His message was simple and clear - no "higher education" was required to understand John's message.

REMEMBER: Do as John admonished, "Follow not that which is evil but that which is good" (III Jn. 11).

JONAH

In the history of Israel (II Kings 14), we find the name of the prophet, Jonah. He is identified as the son of Amittai from the town of Zebulon and his message from God was that their land would be restored to its ancient boundaries under King Jeroboam. The powerful Assyrian empire was in control of the world in those days and its capital was Nineveh. They came to power not long after King Solomon died and the kingdom of Israel was divided. Assyria took control of the northern kingdom and destroyed it, but Jonah prophesied that it would be restored to them.

No wonder, then, it seemed strange to Jonah when God called him to go to Nineveh, the capital of his enemies, and preach to them that God would spare them from His judgment if they would repent. Jonah didn't want them to be spared! If God didn't destroy them, how could his own nation be restored? It all seemed very confusing to Jonah. He didn't understand what God was doing with the nations. So it was that Jonah ran away from God and went the opposite direction of Nineveh.

God used a "great fish" to get Jonah back onto His path and Jonah preached God's message of repentance to the people of Nineveh with reluctance. When they repented and God spared them, Jonah was really out of sorts! He pouted in the hot sun and God caused a plant to grow and shade him one day, but it died the next because of a worm God sent. Job was so angry, he wanted to die, but God chided him saying that if Job wanted to preserve a plant which he had not grown, then God could preserve a great city with many people, if He so chose.

REMEMBER: God told Moses, "I will be gracious to whom I will be gracious, and I will have compassion on whom I will have compassion" (Ex. 33:19). Salvation is of the Lord!

JOSHUA

This name means "salvation" and is spelled "Yeshua" in some places. In the New Testament, we see it as "Jesus".

Joshua, the man, was an aide to Moses as he led the Children of Israel through the wilderness and he demonstrated his faith when he went into Canaan as a spy and returned to encourage the people to enter the land according to God's promise. We know that they were afraid and didn't enter the Promised Land at that time, but wandered aimlessly around in the desert for forty years. Joshua wandered all that way with them and when Moses died, Joshua became their leader.

At last, he was able to lead God's people into the land He had promised them. As with all leaders under God, Joshua had to carry out his responsibility as God directed him. When they did things God's way, they were victorious - otherwise, they went down in defeat. Joshua's greatest equipment for the battles was *"the book of the law"* that God had given His people. Joshua was to do everything that was written there in order to succeed. God said, *"Be strong and of good courage. Be not afraid, neither be thou dismayed, for the Lord, thy God, is with thee whithersoever thou goest"* (Josh. 1:9).

When a crisis arose, Joshua asked God to make the sun stand still - and it did! At the end of his life, Joshua said, *"There failed not ought of any good thing which the Lord had spoken; all came to pass. Not one word has failed"* (Josh. 23:14). Joshua was one of the great leaders of all time because he kept God's Word uppermost in his heart and mind through all the things that happened in his life.

REMEMBER: Like the Psalmist, let us say, "Thy Word have I hid in my heart that I might not sin against Thee" (Ps.119:11).

JOSIAH

Josiah was a king whose reign lasted thirty-one years. The years were marked by independence and religious revival because near the beginning of his reign, Josiah sought for God and cleansed Israel of the gods of idolatry and the places of idolatrous worship. He brought revival and spiritual renewal to Jerusalem and Judah as well as to the cities of the north.

Josiah collected offerings and contributions for the restoration of the temple in Jerusalem which had been neglected for many years. While rebuilding the temple, they found the "book of the law" which Joshua had treasured so highly and Josiah caused it to be read aloud to the people. A great revival broke out among all the people. God's prophet, Jeremiah, was heard and honored in this climate of spiritual renewal. Joseph Holland wrote: "God give us men. A time like this demands strong minds, great hearts, true faith and ready hands; men whom the lust of office does not kill; men whom the spoils of office cannot buy; men who possess opinions and a will; men who have honor; men who will not lie; men who can stand before a demagogue and damn his treacherous flatteries without winking; tall men, sun-crowned, who live above the fog in public duty, and private thinking. For while the rabble with their thumb-worn creeds, their large professions and their little deeds, mingle in selfish strife, freedom weeps, wrong rules the land and waking justice sleeps. God give us men: Men who serve not for selfish booty, but real men, courageous, who flinch not at duty; men of dependable character; men of sterling worth; then wrongs will be redressed, and right will rule the earth. Yes, God give us men!"

REMEMBER: "When the righteous are in power, the people flourish, but when a wicked man rules, the people groan" (Prov. 29:2),

JUDE

The interaction of brothers within a family has been the basis of many sagas. The exchanges between Jesus and His half-brothers was also interesting, no doubt, even though the Bible does not go into detail on this subject. After all, the Bible was written to tell us the story of Jesus, His death and resurrection, not the story of His family life.

We understand from Scripture (Mk. 6:3, Jn. 7:5 and Acts 1:14) that his brothers did not place their faith in Jesus until after His resurrection. We believe that the epistle of James was written by Jesus' brother and Jude calls himself *"the servant of Jesus Christ, brother of James"* so we believe that this man (like James) was the son of Mary and Joseph. James was a leader in the early church and if Jude was a leader, too, he had a spirit of humility about him which is reflected in his writings.

Jude wrote his letter to the churches because there was a tendency to move away from sound doctrine and to allow immorality without conviction. Clearly Jude wrote from a full knowledge of the Old Testament history and teachings. He knew about salvation and the blessings of mercy, peace and love that it brings to the life of the believer. He spoke of the life of believers as a battle for faith in an unfriendly world. He used the stories and teachings of the Jews to present the truths of Christ.

Jude pointed out the certainty with which we can expect God to punish sin. Best of all, however, Jude points out clearly that God can keep us from falling. He can present us *"faultless"* to God the Father when we arrive in glory. We can have *"exceeding joy"* when we come to stand before our God.

REMEMBER: Sin in our lives as believers is not inevitable because Jesus can keep us from falling into its trap.

JUSTIFY

When Job sat on a heap of ashes with boils all over his body, his family and possessions stripped from him, he had just one question on his mind: *"How shall a man be just with God?"* He wasn't asking how to retrieve his lost wealth nor even how to restore his family. Job had an eternal question on his heart concerning his relationship with God.

In the year 1515, an Augustinian monk was lecturing on Romans and he was struck by one verse: *"The just shall live by faith"* (Rom.1:17). Martin Luther's life was never the same after he pondered those words for he began the movement that shook the world, the Reformation. Years later in London, an Anglican missionary read Luther's "Preface to the Epistle to the Romans" and considered the things that had arrested Luther's attention more than 200 years before. John Wesley wrote, "While he was describing the change which God works in the heart through faith in Christ, I felt I did trust in Christ, Christ alone for salvation, and assurance was given me that He had taken away my sins." Romans 5:1 says,

"Being justified by faith, we have peace with God."

God does the justifying and gives us peace when we do our part of confessing our sinfulness and placing our faith in Jesus Christ. We may seem the same outwardly, but inwardly there has been an instantaneous change from "lost sinner" to "justified saint". It takes the rest of our lives to live out what has happened within and even then, we only become like Christ when we see Him face to face. Each day of our Christian life, may we become more like Christ than we were the day before.

REMEMBER: When God "justifies" me, He makes me "just-(as)-if-I" had never sinned.

KING

Kings are nearly as ancient as mankind himself. They are first mentioned in the Bible in Genesis 14 and in the list of kings found there are mentioned the kings of Sodom and Gomorrah.

These cities were built on a fertile delta where a river rich with minerals empties into the Dead Sea from the mountains of what is now Jordan. Sodom and Gomorrah were fertile and wealthy and made a wonderful target for the warring of others who were larger but not so richly endowed. We read that other kings from the Tigris and Euphrates valley came and took all the goods of Sodom and Gomorrah and they captured Abram's nephew, Lot. Abram and his armed servants pursued them all the way to Damascus and defeated them in a night battle. Abram brought back all the goods and Lot with his goods and people. Abram tithed all these goods to the priest Melchizedek, but would not take anything for himself since God was the one who had given them the victory.

The description of the King of kings was not given to Abram but to the Apostle John many years later, but even in his day, Abram understood that God is over all earthly kings. John describes our Heavenly King this way: "I saw ... one like the Son of Man, clothed with a garment down to the foot, and girded about the chest with a golden band. His head and His hair were white like wool, as white as snow; and His eyes were like a flame of fire; And His feet like fine bronze, as if they burned in a furnace; and His voice like the sound of many waters. And He had in His right hand seven stars; and ... His countenance was as the sun shineth in its strength." (Rev. 1:13-16). This is Jesus in His heavenly glory and power!

REMEMBER: Jesus is the only one who is found worthy to be King of kings and King of our lives.

KNEES

There are many sayings about our knees - "the knees go first", "bring him to his knees", and "prayer bones" are a few of the ways we use this word. Encouragement is called *"strengthening the weak knees"*. Very often in the Bible, the idea of submission is conveyed with the picture of kneeling before God and this is right, for we are not worthy to stand in the presence of the King of kings. The humility we express by kneeling is appropriate when we come to God in prayer.

Jesus Himself knelt in the Garden of Gethsemane as he struggled with the agony of His death, coming to the place of submission to His Father's will. Jesus had prayed to His Father before - sometimes standing with His eyes raised to heaven, but to show His submission, He knelt in prayer in Gethsemane.

For us, too, it is possible to pray in other positions - with or without our eyes closed - that is not a hindrance to prayer. God hears the cry of our hearts wherever we are - whatever our body's position. Yet, for many such as George Washington, it is a practice of life to kneel before God in prayer. He knelt in the early days of the Continental Congress in Philadelphia and later, he knelt in the snow beside the Potomac River seeking God's protection and guidance for himself and his war-weary men. His humble, trusting faith has brought blessing on our country through the ensuing years. Washington's diary records the humility of his heart before God even while accepting responsibility as a leader of men - yes, even the leader of a nation.

REMEMBER: We will do well to follow the example of those through the centuries who knelt in humility and submission before God, our Heavenly Father, who is worthy of our worship (Phil. 2:9-11).

KNOCK

We use this word in so many ways, it would be hard to list them all. We can knock at a door; our car engine can knock; a boxer can knock out his opponent; a worker can knock off early; a salesman can knock off the price.

In the Bible, we are told to ASK for what we need, to SEEK and we will find, to KNOCK and find an opening. God encourages us to speak to Him about things that concern us and then to seek His answers. Still, if we have not received our requests, we are to knock and keep on knocking for He has promised to open the door for us to move forward. This growing intensity is honored by God when we seek His blessing and His will for our lives.

In Revelation 3:20 we see Jesus doing the knocking for He stands outside a closed door, seeking to find entrance - waiting for someone to open the door to Him. He is calling at the same time. He says, *"If any man hear My voice"* and we see that He is knocking with the same intensity with which He encourages us to knock - all but demanding an answer.

Jesus stands outside the door of our hearts and knocks patiently, repeatedly and hopefully, expecting that at any moment, the door will swing wide so He can enter. He promises to come in if we will open the door. We must remember, however, that the latch is on the inside where only we can open the door. Jesus does not come with a battering ram to splinter the door and enter your heart and life. He waits for you to respond to His persistent, pleading knock, and to open the door. THEN, He will come in and your fellowship will be sweet.

REMEMBER: Many voices call to us, but the voice of the Savior is sweet and loving. "Today if you will hear My voice, harden not your hearts," Jesus said.

KNOWLEDGE

"What do you know?" we call out to one another in cheery greeting. No one begins to recount all the knowledge he possesses in response to that invitation!

We know a lot about a lot of things. When that knowledge is classified, we call it science. When we use our knowledge to good advantage, we call it wisdom. There are everyday things we need to know and there are eternal questions for which we need to know the answers.

Adam and Eve got into trouble because they wanted to know something God had told them not to find out. The devil tempted them to eat of the Tree of the Knowledge of Good and Evil - they didn't know one from the other for they had experienced only good. They weren't convinced that God knew best for them, so they tasted of the tree and thought they would become like God. Their punishment has fallen on us all.

Knowledge is certainly not always bad, however, for God instructs us to pursue knowledge and understanding so that we can know the fear of the Lord and believe what He teaches us. Solomon summed up the whole of life by saying,

"Fear God and keep His commandments; for this is the whole duty of man"(Eccl. 12:31).

We must know God's commandments in order to keep them! That kind of knowledge will lead us to assurance—to *"know that all things work together for good to them that love God"*. To seek knowledge without God is a contradiction in terms for He is the fountain of all knowledge.

REMEMBER: May our lives be an open book speaking loud and clear of the mercy and grace of God to all who will "read" what we are writing there.

KNOWN

- "... that Thy way may be known upon earth" (Ps. 67:3).
- "The Lord hath made known His salvation (Ps. 98:2).
- "Thou hast searched me and known me" (Ps. 139:11).
- "Even a child is known by his doings" (Prov. 20:11).
- "I know My sheep and am known of Mine" (Jn. 10:14).
- "Known unto God are all His works" (Acts 15:18).

These and many other verses of Scripture use the word "known" for the Bible is a book of certainties and assurance.

A well-known preacher received a letter from a lady in a town where he was to speak. She enclosed her picture so that he would recognize her and speak with her while in her city. They happened to reach to church at the same time, and he spoke to her. She was delighted to see that he knew her on sight and that her effort in writing and sending a picture had been fruitful.

How like her we are! In this world with its millions of people, we often feel that we are "lost in the crowd", but there is no time but that God knows where we are and all that is happening to us. Paul wrote, *"If any man love God, the same is known of Him"* (I Cor. 8:3).

His knowledge of us is complete, individual and personal. It includes all of our circumstances as well as a loving parental delight in us. *"To be known of God"* means a great deal more than simply being recognized - it means that we belong to Him and He cares for us kindly and sympathetically.

REMEMBER: "My Father watches over me, His eye is never dim, At morning, at noon, at evening time I'm always known of Him!"

LABOR

Labor is well known to all of us. A life would not be complete without work. It produces both tears and joy and it can be done for the sake of love as well as from need. Labor pains produce the birth of a child and in this case, too, there is both joy and sorrow mingled together. God created work as part of the curse on the earth when Adam and Eve sinned, yet Solomon in his wisdom wrote, *"In all labor there is profit"* (Prov. 14:23) and his advice was, *"Whatsoever thy hand findeth to do, do it with your might"* (Eccl. 9:10). So, instead of avoiding work, wisdom tells us to embrace it and lend our strength and energy to accomplish it. God gave us work to do, and there is real pleasure in doing it. Too much leisure time can lead to sin and ultimately to a miserable life.

We should thank God for every day in which we have something that must be done. It gives our lives meaning and purpose which nothing else can do. We learn things in the course of carrying out our work that we learn in no other way - things like self-control, diligence, contentment and many other things. Adam Clark worked on his Bible commentary for forty years. Webster spent thirty-six years working on his dictionary. Milton rose before dawn each morning to write his poetry while other activites did not creat a conflict. Gibson spent twenty-six years writing "The Decline and Fall of the Roman Empire", but it towers as a monument to careful research and dedication. Bryant re-wrote one of his poems one hundred times before it was published in order to attain complete beauty and perfection of expression. These men all enjoyed their work and gave their energies and talents to it without reservation. But, the best work of all is the work of the Lord.

REMEMBER: If you want to leave footprints in the sands of time - wear workshoes!

LAMENTATIONS

In his Old Testament book, we read the story of how Jeremiah was sent by God to warn the people of Jerusalem of coming destruction unless they repented of their wicked lifestyle and turned back to God. Jeremiah grieved over the message and over the lack of response from his people. They refused to hear God's call to repentance, and it broke the prophet's heart. His sorrow took the form of tears and lamentings.

God's judgment is a sorrowful thing ... and it is sure. When Jeremiah saw the destruction of the city he loved and saw the plight of his people, Jeremiah could not keep from crying out loud. He confessed the sins of the people in their behalf. Many were bitter against God, but Jeremiah reminded them, *"The Lord is good unto them that wait for Him, to the soul that seeketh Him"* (Jer. 3:24). He reminded them that it was only by God's grace that they were not completely consumed.

About 400 A.D., a man named Chrysostom stood before the Roman emperor. The monarch roared, "You will die at my hand." This Christian man, Chrysostom, said that he could do nothing to harm him. The emperor threatened to take his riches, but the prisoner replied, "My treasures are in heaven." The threats continued with, "I will exile you from your country" to which Chrysostom replied that his citizenship was in heaven. Frustrated, the emperor could only listen as his captive repeated, "There is nothing you can take from me and nothing you can do to harm me." How different his story is from the people of Jerusalem in Jeremiah's day.

REMEMBER: When sin abounds, God's grace abounds even more. Let us look to Him for hope and help. "His compassions fail not. They are new every morning; great is thy faithfulness" (Lam. 3:22-23).

LARGENESS

This unusual word is found only once in the Bible — in I Kings 4:29 where it says,

> *"God gave Solomon wisdom and very much understanding and largeness of heart."*

We often say it this way, "That man has a big heart." We refer to his generosity and love for others and it is not in proportion to his education or the greatness of his mind.

People are often educated beyond their ability to use their knowledge wisely. This makes them nothing more than "educated fools". Solomon was different, however, for God gave him knowledge, wisdom AND a big heart. He never lost "the human touch".

A world famous Mayo Clinic physician was asked what inspired him to become a doctor. His reply was, "It was the deep and lasting impression made on my heart by a family doctor who ministered to my younger brother when I was a boy. It was clear that he not only had great skill as a physician, but he had a loving heart that made him warm and friendly, dedicated to his patient. His good judgment saved my brother's life and I was compelled to follow his example."

Learning is very desirable, but we need more than facts - we also need wisdom to make our education effective in dealing with people. It has been said that "a little knowledge is a dangerous thing". True! It is easy to use "data" as a dagger!

"An understanding heart and mind, I pray, Lord, give to me; As tender as the heart of Him who walked in Galilee!" (Anon.)

REMEMBER: Learning only finds its highest level of usefulness when it is accompanied by largeness of heart.

LAUGH

When God told Abraham that the aging Sarah would have a son, she laughed at the very idea. She knew her own body and it was clear that she was past the child-bearing years of her life. It sounded ridiculous - so she laughed!

God will laugh at those who mock Him and plot to rebel against Him. His laugh will be in derision of their puny efforts. He laughs at those who plot wickedness against the righteous, too. In fact, God laughs at all who fail to call Him Lord. How terrible it would be to hear that laugh directed at yourself - the futility of taking a stand against God is laughable indeed!

We don't read of Jesus laughing, but we are told that others laughed at Him. He seemed too humble a person - poor and homeless, yet He claimed such great powers for Himself - like the ability to give life to the daughter of a ruler who came to him seeking help. More often than laughing, Jesus wept over those who were rejecting Him and His message.

Comedians are among the highest paid entertainers because people find it important that someone make them laugh. Solomon had something different in mind, however, when he said, "A merry heart doeth good like a medicine" (Prov.17:22). An old adage says, "Laugh and the world laughs with you; cry, and you cry alone." Actually, it is not laughter we really need - it is joy. That is the deep, abiding happiness that gives us the ability to laugh easily and often. Joy is a fruit of the Holy Spirit and it comes when He fills our thoughts and minds. Jesus didn't offer us laughter, but He offered us joy:

"These things have I spoken unto you, that my joy might remain in you" (Jn15:11).

REMEMBER: The joy of the Lord is our strength.

LAW

It has always been true that many among us seem unable to bear the restraint of law upon us. The rebellious nature of mankind makes us push and tug at the laws that surround us. How futile! No matter how much we dislike the law of gravity, we cannot change it. We learn to cope with it and to use a higher power (like the laws of aerodynamics) to overcome it for a while, but we cannot cancel it - it is one of God's laws which He has made.

We live with many such laws of nature and of life every day of our lives. These basic laws cannot be broken without paying the price. They cannot be broken without them breaking us. God gave His laws for life and spiritual matters in the books of Moses - the first five books of our Bibles. The summary is found in the Ten Commandments which tells us what good and evil are - and they tell us to do good, not evil (Exodus 20).

As world population increased, governments began to make laws to handle the many situations and problems that arose. Roman law, English law and American laws are based on God's Word. Many of the great legal minds were steeped in the truth of God's Word and formulated the laws of their nation accordingly.

We must teach children to obey the laws of the universe and the laws of the land. Life is made up of obeying - working in concert with God's laws instead of contradicting them. The sun, moon and stars obey God's laws and shine in their places year after year as God has set them in the heavens. God's laws are made so they can function wonderfully.

REMEMBER: God gave us laws because He loves us and wants the best for us. We show Him our love by obeying His words. Jesus said, "If a man love me, he will keep my words" (Jn. 14:23).

LAWLESS

Many people today seem to think that being permissive is not only their right, but also a good thing. "Test the limits," they preach. "Expand your mind." God, on the other hand, sees this permissiveness as lawlessness and labels it as such. Paul wrote to Timothy and said,

"The law is good, and is not made for the righteous man but for the lawless and disobedient" (I Tim. 1:19).

How true! A good person freely does good things, so he has no need of laws to direct his actions. However, the disobedient person must be told what he can and cannot do in order to keep our society intact. Those who insist on having their own way disregard God and their fellow human beings and they break both the laws of God and of government.

After Moses and Joshua died and the Children of Israel were in the Promised Land, they had no appointed leader - no civil authority and *"every man did that which was right in his own eyes"*. Chaos reigned. God punished them repeatedly as long as they chose to suit themselves at all costs. The punishment would remind the people of God and His ways and they would repent, then soon the cycle would begin again. How like us they were!

The anti-Christ who is to come and lead the world in rebellion against God is called *"the lawless one"* for he will direct everyone against the good that God has set before us. He will make good seem evil, and evil good. But Jesus came *"not to destroy the law, but to fulfill it"*.

REMEMBER: To be like Jesus - that is the greatest goal for our lives.

LEVITICUS

We look back 2,000 years to the days of Jesus' life on earth. About the same number of years before, Jacob and his wife, Leah, had a son and they called him "Levi". Leah knew that Jacob loved Rachel more than he loved her and she hoped that this son would unite them in a new and greater way. Levi means "joined". From this son came the long line of Levitical priests whom God established among His people to carry out the sacrifices of the Law of Moses.

The instructions for the priesthood are listed in the Book of Leviticus. It tells of sacrifices, feasts, and fasts for although the Hebrew people can be very sorrowful, so also they can rejoice and celebrate at the appropriate times.

This book foreshadows the Gospel truth of the Lamb of God slain for the sins of the whole world. Holiness is the key word and it tells mankind how to gain access into the presence of God. Good works are not the means of pleasing God, but rather we are to place our faith in the sacrifice that God has given.

Leviticus is not a book of history, but a book of laws for worship that set Israel apart from every other nation on earth. Five feasts are laid out to be held each year for this is no solemn book of legalism. God loves to celebrate and He taught His people to celebrate with great feasts and joyous gatherings. Passover, Pentecost, Trumpets and Yom Kippur (the Day of Atonement) are followed by the Feast of Tabernacles which is a fall holiday when for two days, the people meet and eat and enjoy one another. Moses said they were *"to proclaim liberty throughout all the land unto the inhabitants thereof"* *(Lev. 25:10)*.

REMEMBER: Through Jesus' sacrifice of Himself for our sakes, we too can have liberty and be glad.

LIBERTY

Freedom from restraint and oppression - that is liberty. The rights of citizens are called "civil liberties" - areas where the people of a nation have freedom to exercise their choices. A sailor gets "liberty" when he can leave the ship and the discipline of service for a brief time.

Americans have loved liberty from the earliest days on this continent. The people had known oppression as wickedness and lawlessness had run rampant in England during Elizabethan days. They were put to death for reading the Bible or teaching their children to say the 23rd Psalm. Meanwhile, corrupt government officials took their crops and plundered their homes for anything of value. They had no recourse - no one to "proclaim liberty" to them. So, in the new world, they wanted freedom - liberty to live as they saw fit without interference from their leaders except where civil order had to be maintained.

Worse than the bondage of a corrupt government, however, is the bondage to sin that so many liberty-loving Americans know only too well. How the habits of sin cling to us and govern our behavior to do things we would not naturally do. And how deadly the consequences! When sin rules over us, we have no good thing to look forward to and we cannot free ourselves.

Only in Christ is there hope to find true freedom and the liberty to live as God intended - according to His laws and truth. How alive we are when the chains of sin no longer hold us in their power. We are scarred by sin, but Christ came "to set at liberty them that are bruised".

REMEMBER: If your soul is sick of sin, turn to Jesus! He offers you life and liberty beyond anything you've ever known.

LILY

How lovely are the lilies that line our churches at Easter. They remind us of God's handiwork, the beauty of all He has given us. The waxy, pure white of the lily speaks of our Savior's beauty and holiness. Although many flowers have brilliant colors, the lily is snow white and it blooms in the spring when the whole world is coming to life again after the long winter season. Some use lilies for funerals to remind us that from death will spring new life "in due season".

The lily is a resurrection flower - it grows from a bulb that appears dead and dry, having no life at all. Yet, when planted, it sprouts and flowers with the spring rains. God's promises about Israel are like that. He said that Israel would "grow as a lily" - life sprouting from a bulb that seems dead.

Jesus told us to *"consider the lilies, how they grow. They toil not neither do they spin; and yet I say unto you, that Solomon in all his glory was not arrayed like one of these"* (Lk. 12:27). We're to take a close look at the lilies and think about the God who made them.

Their glory is magnificent, yet they are here one day and soon cut down and thrown into the fire. God is generous with the beauty He places on this earth. It doesn't have to last long, nor have a great place of honor. God strews beauty across the fields and meadows with a generous hand so we can see it and think of Him. He wants the lily to remind us that we are more valuable to Him than a simple lily, yet He cares for the lily and brings it to fruition supplying all that it needs. Won't He do at least that much for us?

REMEMBER: The lilies of the field are there to remind us that God delights in making our lives beautiful and He will supply all that it takes to make them so.

LOVE

Love is the very character of God - He cannot be unloving. Those of us who belong to Him are to reflect His love in our world. Harold Kesley has translated the Love Chapter (I Cor. 13) this way:

"Though I may be able to speak French, Spanish and Japanese, and even rap with the angels, if I haven't love, my speech isn't anything more than a broken guitar or a scratched record. I may preach like Billy Graham, have the brains of Einstein, I may have all the faith needed to put a Volkswagen into a phone booth, but if I don't have love, I'm nothing. I can give the shirt off my back and discipline myself by breaking my old albums, but if I don't have love, it won't do me any good.

"Love is tolerant and tender. Love isn't stuck up or uptight. Love isn't cynical, snooty or touchy. Love isn't pessimistic. Love doesn't lie in the gutter or hunt for gossip, but it is made happy by the truth. Love never cops out. Faith, hope and love never fail. They outlast life and the universe. People talk, talk, talk, but seldom get things done. Money may buy the world, but we can't seem to hang onto it. Looking at life is like looking in mirrors at the carnival - things are twisted, distorted and ridiculous, but some day God will open our eyes and we'll be able to see life as God intended it to be. Love is the greatest!"

REMEMBER: Jesus told us to love our neighbor like we love ourselves ... and no one ever hated himself!

LUKE

One of the apostles was Luke, the beloved physician. He was a Gentile, and he had been trained in medicine in the great school of Alexandria in Egypt. He came on the scene late and found Jesus after hearing about Him from many who had known Him. As a doctor, Luke wanted to see this man who healed EVERYONE who came to him. Doctors have their "failures" when the patient dies, but here was a man who healed everyone He touched. This was amazing to Luke and he set out to find Jesus.

Although he did not have a personal experience of the Jewish life, he took in all that he saw - trying to grasp the obviously great significance of the life of Christ. Later, Luke travelled with Paul on some of his missionary journeys. They went to many cities where only a small part of the population were Jews. Luke understood the Greek culture and it was to them that he addressed his Gospel. Greeks loved beauty, culture, orations and philosophy, and Luke was well fitted to address them since he was highly educated in their culture.

Luke presents Jesus in particular as the Son of Man - God manifested in human flesh, experiencing life as we know it. Luke tells us of Jesus' birth and how miraculous it was - how fitting that a physician should convey these truths to us! He traces Jesus' growth and development through childhood and he tells of His amazing discourse with the leaders of the temple when He was only twelve. Luke tells us that Jesus worked with His hands, became weary after a long day, wept over Jerusalem, knelt in prayer and experienced suffering as any man would.

REMEMBER: Jesus was a normal man, except that he lived His life without sin. He became sin for us so that we can have the righteousness of God.

MAN

Feelings of unworthiness often flood the human mind. Don't you wonder why God bothers with us at all? We have proved throughout the centuries that we cannot be trusted to obey His laws or bring Him pleasure, yet He loves us and keeps forgiving our waywardness. We alone, of all creation, can consider His love and understand that He truly cares about the human race.

A Christian man (a Christian woman, too!) is to be an imitator of Jesus Christ. There is nothing "wimpish" about being a Christian man for Christ was masculine and strong, working with His hands in Joseph's carpenter shop. He led His disciples with great authority, yet was still able to bow His head and speak to His Heavenly Father with great humility, giving honor to His Father.

Jesus treated women with respect and gave them a place of dignity and worth in spite of the lowly place they held in many societies. Still, Jesus made it clear that a man's responsibility is to be the leader of his home and family, his wife and children accepting his leadership with the same humility they have before God, knowing that he must answer to God for the way he manages family affairs.

Many times in Scripture, the word "man" actually means both men and women and there is no different standard of life held up for women than that required of men even though their responsibilities and functions are different. Women, too, come to God through faith in Jesus Christ and are expected to *"live godly in this present world"*.

REMEMBER: If any man (ANYONE) be in Christ, he is a new creature; old things are passed away, behold all things are become new" (I Cor. 5:17).

MAGICIANS

As far back as we have any knowledge of mankind - almost back to the Garden of Eden, we have records of magic, magicians and people who believed in them. To those who refuse to honor God as the Creator, it must seem like "magic" for Him to have made something out of nothing. That's what magicians try to simulate wherever they go. Yet we know that everything comes from something in our own experience; therefore, the Creation of the universe out of nothing becomes even more amazing. When Satan or his followers try to imitate what God has done, it becomes "magic" and follows Satan's plan to "become like God".

There were magicians in Egypt in Joseph's day (Gen. 41). When Joseph was in prison, the king had a dream which his magicians could not interpret. God had oftentimes before given Joseph the meaning of dreams and Joseph had the reputation that he could successfully interpret dreams. Joseph accomplished this in God's power not by magic, so his interpretations were always right. So, when the king needed someone to interpret his dream and his magicians couldn't do it, he called on Joseph and brought him out of prison to interpet for him. The Pharoah honored Joseph by making him second man in the kingdom.

Moses, too, worked miracles by God's power. The Egyptian magicians imitated these miracles, but in the end, they failed and acknowledged that Moses' miracles were "the finger of God". Daniel met magicians in Babylon in his day. Again, they could not interpret the king's dream and God gave His man the ability to explain the meaning of the vision he had been given.

REMEMBER: God's power accomplishes the supernatural, but when the devil imitates that power, it is empty magic - trickery done by the power of Satan himself which cannot match the power of God.

MAJESTY

This term is used in addressing royalty or in describing the grandeur of a landscape. Most appropriately, it is used in connection with God. *"He is clothed with majesty,"* we read in Psalm 93. *"I will speak of Thy glorious honor, of Thy majesty, and of Thy wondrous works,"* rings Psalm 145. Peter wrote lovingly in the New Testament of the years he spent with Jesus, *"We were eyewitnesses of His majesty"* (II Peter 1:16).

In our efforts today to emphasize the love of God, we have lost something of His majesty to our detriment. God loves us in an intimate way, but we must never let ourselves think of Him as being weak, inadequate, ineffective or pathetic as we sometimes are. We are limited in every way, but He is not limited in any way! He is not limited by time for He is eternal. He is not limited by space for He is present everywhere. He is not limited in knowledge for He knows everything. He is not limited in power for there is nothing He cannot do. So even though He is our personal friend, He is full of power, glory and majesty.

> *"Where can I go from His presence? If I ascend up into heaven, Thou art there. If I descend into the uttermost parts of the sea, behold! Thou art there. If I take the wings of the morning, even there shall Thy hand lead me" (Psalm 139).*

> *"Who has measured the waters in the hollow of His hand, and marked off the heavens by the span, and calculated the dust of earth by the measure, and weighed the mountains in a balance, and the hills in a pair of scales?" (Isaiah 40:12).*

REMEMBER: "Great is the Lord and greatly to be praised."

MARK

It appears that Mark, who accompanied Paul and Barnabas to Antioch, was a man of few words and a lot of action. Peter had brought him to Jesus and those two had a special relationship which lasted through the years. Mark was a great help to Paul, too, so he was well-liked by the leaders of the early church.

Mark's ability to help those in places of leadership sprang from his understanding of Jesus' ministry for Mark wrote, "Even the Son of Man came not to be ministered unto but to minister and to give His life a ransom for many" (Mark 10:45). Then Mark wrote of all the things that Jesus did for others. This was the guiding light of his life and Mark, too, served others and ministered to their needs (Mark 10:45).

This emphasis on serving and on Christ as a servant had a special appeal to the Romans of Mark's day for they had many servants and they knew what it took to be a good servant - obedience and submission to the master's will. Jesus lived a life of obedience to His Father's will, submitting to His commands in all that He did. Since the lineage of a servant is not important, Mark does not give the line of David from which Jesus came as the King. Mark writes only of His adult life, beginning with His baptism in the River Jordan, and his Gospel is a story of action - swift and decisive. It seemed to Mark that the time he spent with Jesus passed quickly and was filled with activity. The conclusion of his Gospel continues in the same vein -

"Go ye into all the world and preach the gospel to every creature" (Mark 16;15).

REMEMBER: When we help others, we are emulating Jesus Christ, Son of Man and servant to the helpless and needy people of this world.

MATTHEW

This name means "gift of God" although while the Gospel writer was still collecting taxes, it seemed incongruous. The taxgatherers were very unfair and had gained a reputation for cheating people with the approval of the Romans. So, this Jew was inflicting oppressive taxes on his fellow countrymen with the blessing of the Roman conquerors. No wonder people held a great deal of hostility against him and the others who collected taxes. When he found Jesus and followed him, however, Matthew became a man whose name held a positive meaning - "gift of God". History says that he travelled as a missionary and died in a foreign land.

The Gospel according to Matthew was written to the Jews in particular and it gives the lineage by which Jesus laid claim to the throne of David. He took for granted that his readers knew what had happened when Jesus preached in Galilee. He took up the story found at the end of the Old Testament and carried God's message forward by writing about Jesus as the fulfillment of the prophecies given hundreds of years before. God's silence of 400 years was broken when Matthew began to write of the Messiah descending from David. Joseph of Nazareth was a man with a rightful claim to that throne, but instead the Roman conquerors had set up Herod as the king of Israel. In spite of Jesus' credentials, however, the Jews did not see Him as the Messiah that Matthew proclaimed. They seemed to prefer the domination of the Romans rather than to receive Jesus as their Messiah. They were confused for they thought their coming king would reign over all the earth. Little did they know that His kingdom is yet to come - and Jesus will reign!

REMEMBER: When He comes in majesty, every eye shall see Him and every knee will bow before Him giving honor and glory to His name.

MEASURE

The Bible uses this word in four different forms. The first has reference to the meal offering and the dimensions of the Old Testament tabernacle and the temple. Meal for the offerings was always to be the exact same amount - no more, no less. All the curtains of the sanctuaries were also to be exactly the same size (Ex. 26:2). In these two cases, it was important to God that the amounts not reflect the measure of devotion of the worshipper or the worker - He did not allow for skimping (a short measure) nor for an expression of extra devotion on the part of the worker or the worshipper.

Of course, in business, products are measured in the normal day's activity, and the Bible uses this word in regard to the distribution of crops produced in the Holy Land. Zechariah was told to measure the city of Jerusalem when he rebuilt the walls, Ezekiel was to measure the temple area when he rebuilt the temple and an angel is said to have a golden rod by which to measure the the New Jerusalem which will be the capitol of the world when Christ reigns during the Millenium.

It is also said that we "take the measure of a man (or woman)", but the Corinthians measured themselves by themselves (II Cor. 10:12) which was unwise. God's standard is the only reliable measure we can use for our lives. His Word teaches us what we need to know about His requirements. Our stature as a Christian is often measured by the faith we live by in our daily lives. Paul was given *"a thorn in the flesh"* so that he would not be exalted *"above measure"* since he was such a great leader in the days of the early Church (II Cor. 12:7).

REMEMBER: How we measure up as people of faith is important to God - He cares about measures, dimensions and sizes.

MEASURELESS

The very word indicates our inability to comprehend the limits of a thing. **We can measure** distance, time, weight, rate of movement, and many of these are amazing! Astronomers **can** measure the size of the universe; scientists **can** calculate the weight of a mountain; the speed at which light travels **is** measurable even if amazing, so we (like the Psalmist) wonder, *"What is man that Thou art mindful of him?"* (Ps. 8:4).

Still, we cannot measure infinity ... nor can we comprehend eternity. By their very definition, these things are measureless. Solomon said, "Will God dwell on the earth? Behold the heaven and heaven of heavens cannot contain Thee!" What is there in the human race that makes God care about us? If we say that God cares about everything He has created, we emphasize His infinite love. If we remember that we are "made in His image", we emphasize His great power in creation. No wonder He loves us — we are His creation which He made because He wanted us.

That explains God's warm, unlimited welcome to us to come into His presence and to be His friends! Again and again, God pled with His chosen people throughout history to come near to Him and to walk with Him. Those who came (like Abraham, David, Enoch and many others) were ALWAYS received without barriers and with many attendant blessings.

It is no wonder, then, that there are certain things that God expects of us. Isaiah wrote, "Thus saith the high and lofty One that inhabiteth eternity, whose name is Holy; I will dwell in the high and holy place, with him also that is of a contrite and humble spirit" (Isa. 57:15). Even though we are welcome in God's presence, we cannot enter there with pride in our hearts.

REMEMBER: There is no place for human pride in the presence of our infinite, eternal God.

MEAT

More than the flesh of animals which we use for food, this word indicates the heart of things - the best part. The Bible speaks of meat many times and it often refers to all of the food which God supplies rather than to animal flesh (meat) only. In Genesis, God told Adam and Eve that he had given them grain and fruit to be "meat" for them. Their diet contained no meat as we know it until later, after the Fall. Their food was simple and plain as has so often been the case with God's choicest servants.

John the Baptist had locusts and wild honey to eat as he lived in the wilderness proclaiming the coming King. When Jesus fed the 5,000, they ate bread and fish and what was gathered as left-overs was called "seven baskets of meat". So often, however, we think of dining elegantly and richly as a sign of God's blessing, but appetites tend to take over our lives, if indulged.

"Thy words were found and I did eat them, and Thy word was unto me the joy and rejoicing of my heart" (Jer. 15:16).

"I have esteemed the words of his mouth more than my necessary food" (Job 23:12).

Jesus said that His meat was to do the will of His Father. Fasting helps the believer to remember that spiritual things are more important even than our daily food.

Paul referred to the pagan practice of offering meat to idols when he said that he would no longer eat meat, if others thought he was involved in such idolatry. The meat offered to idols was unchanged as far as Paul was concerned, but if it were a problem for others if he ate such meat, he would deny himself.

REMEMBER: Jesus said, "If any man will come after Me, let him deny himself and take up his cross daily, and follow Me" (Luke 9:23).

MENE

This ancient word is found in only one place in Scripture (Daniel 5). It is part of the warning of God to Belshazzar, King of Babylon, when he hosted a dinner for his generals to celebrate the greatness of their kingdom.

Years before that banquet, Babylon had captured the Children of Israel and had taken the best of the young people and removed them to their own country as servants. They had conquered the entire world (at least so it seemed) and Belshazzar had built the Hanging Gardens - one of the seven wonders of the world. He had constructed a magnificent city as his capitol and every brick in the extensive waterway was marked with his name. Daniel, Shadrach, Meshach and Abednego were his servants.

In the midst of the drunken banquet, God's disgust with their sin and pride reached the level of intolerance and He sent an armless hand to write His warning on the wall of that great hall. The king was sober in an instant for he knew that this was some kind of apparition from the realm of the supernatural which appeared to bring him a message, but none of his magicians could tell him what it said. Belshazzar had the mightiest army in the world... but he was afraid. Frantic, he accepted someone's suggestion to send for Daniel who had interpreted dreams for him. MENE MENE, God had said. *"God is counting and He remembers,"* was the ominous message. *"Your kingdom is divided and given to the Medes and the Persians."* Finally, their sin was judged and that very night, the enemy poured into their city through the bed of a diverted river and killed Belshazzar and his leaders in that same banquet hall. They learned too late that *"your sin will find you"*.

REMEMBER: "Be not deceived, God is not mocked, for whatsoever a man sows, that will he also reap" (Gal. 6:7).

MICAH

This name is only one of the many forms of the name Michael which means, *"He is like Jehovah"*. At least seven men in the Bible had this name or one of its forms. The Prophet Micah lived and spoke during the reigns of kings from Jotham to Hezekiah and most of those kings were good and obedient to God. Micah lived about 700 B.C. near the Philistine border on a plain about thirty miles southwest of Jerusalem. God gave him a message of warning - that Israel's sin would bring about destruction, but God would eventually restore her out of His great mercy.

The Children of Israel lived in the Promised Land in those days, but they had allowed the wickedness of the Canaanites to permeate their lives and God warned them that He would punish them for this sinfulness. Micah presents in a nutshell what is required of people who would live for God - *"... to do justly, to love mercy and to walk humbly with God."*

Micah is the prophet who tells us that Jesus will be born in Bethlehem and predicts His coming kingdom while reminding us that He *"has been from of old, from everlasting"*. So, while Micah is speaking to the people of his day and prophesying of the Messiah's coming to reign in the last days, he is also teaching us how to live for God in any day or time. His words were quoted by Jesus to His disciples when He sent them out to witness of Himself, warning them not to place their trust in people, but to expect help from God alone. Micah reminds us that God will hear us when we call upon Him. Micah repeats that God will do all that He has promised - for Abraham, for Jacob ... and for us.

REMEMBER: The Apostle Paul reiterates this truth: "He that hath begun a good work in you will perform it until the day of Jesus Christ."

MOUTH

Most often we think of what goes into our mouths whenever we think of our mouth at all, but the Bible more often portrays our mouths as the revealer of what is in our hearts. *"Out of the abundance of the mouth the heart speaketh"* (Matt. 12:34), we read. Proverbs tells us that the mouths of fools *"pour out foolishness"* whereas *"the mouth of the righteous speaketh wisdom"*. God is greatly concerned with the things that come from our mouths and constantly warns against allowing pride or wickedness to flow from our lips.

God made our mouths - along with the rest of us - and He made them in order that we could give Him praise and glory. No wonder He is offended when we glorify ourselves (pride) or speak words that fail to praise His holy name! He waits to hear what we will say to others about Him before He claims us as His own before His Father in Heaven for He will not acknowledge us unless we acknowledge Him before our peers. If we refuse to acknowledge Him as God in our lives, He will deny us before His Father as well (Matt. 10:32-33).

Our mouths not only bring us to God in the first place, they also make it possible for us to draw near to God for when we praise Him and give Him the honor that is due to Him, we open the path directly into the presence of God and we can come *"boldly before the throne of grace"*. There we are free to express our feelings and thoughts without restraint and there we can ask Him for anything that is not contrary to His will as revealed in His Word. No wonder the Psalmist prayed, *"Set a watch, O Lord, before my mouth. Keep the door of my lips"* (Ps. 141:3).

REMEMBER: We can pray as the Psalmist did, "Let the words of my mouth ... be acceptable in Thy sight, O Lord" (Ps. 19:14).

NATHANIEL

One of the twelve disciples was named Nathaniel which means "gift of God". Many before him, and many since, have carried this wonderful name. Philip brought this Nathaniel to Jesus immediately after Jesus had called him to follow Him. Philip knew that this was the man foretold in the Scriptures who would come and fulfill the words of God. Jesus saw Nathaniel coming and said that he was a man who was not a deceiver - *"a man in whom there is no guile"* (Jn. 1:47). He also underlined the fact that Nathaniel was an Israelite - one who was chosen of God. Many of the people of Israel were Israelites in name only and did not commit their lives to follow God.

Nathaniel came from Cana which was near Nazareth; however, the people of Cana were more educated and concerned themselves with intellectual pursuits. Nazareth, at the time of Jesus, was a Roman garrison and certainly not known for being the home of intellectuals.

Nathaniel was amazed him to hear Jesus speak intimately of him when they had not previously met, and considered it to be a sign that Jesus truly was the Son of God. He did not ponder or question, but immediately acknowledged Jesus for who He was. Then, he followed Jesus as He travelled and taught throughout Galilee. Nathaniel saw the miracles that Jesus did - how He healed all who came to Him and spoke to the people with great love and concern. After Jesus returned to heaven, Nathaniel was a witness to all the world concerning the things he had seen and heard. Nathaniel was the "gift of God", not only to his family, but also to all those who heard him speak of Jesus.

REMEMBER: We, also, can believe in Jesus without delay. Then, no matter what our names are, we can be a "gift of God", too.

NEHEMIAH

Nehemiah lived in about 430 B.C. and was one of the last to record the history of the Jews before the 400 years of silence which preceded the birth of Jesus. He was a prophet as was Ezra, but Ezra's job was to build the temple in Jerusalem whereas Nehemiah was sent by God to build the walls of the city. The walls were their security as they dwelt there at the "crossroads of the world". Nehemiah was born in captivity and he served the king as his "cupbearer" (a position of honor) in the greatest nation of his day. He was loyal to his captors and was trusted with the delicate and dangerous job of tasting the king's food to ascertain that it was free from poison. In spite of his high position, Nehemiah was sad about the condition of Israel, his homeland, and he could not help letting it show in his face.

Ezra had gone back to build the temple, but the work was slow and hard. In the course of their labor, they found the scroll which contained the law of Moses. It had been "misplaced" for years and the people had not heard God's Word for a long time - some of them were too young ever to have heard it read aloud. Ezra called all the people together in front of the water gate and began to read the Scriptures to them. When they heard God's Word, they stood all morning in reverence and awe as it was read, then they raised their hands and bowed their heads, worshipping the Lord as they understood His Word. "Amen, amen," they said. "So be it." Nehemiah heard of this and wanted to make the city secure for the people who had rebuilt the temple. His heart longed to be in Jerusalem with them. He, too, wanted to hear God's Word and to worship Him. So the king allowed him to go and gave him materials and authority to do what he so longed to do (Neh. 1:7-8).

REMEMBER: God has work for each of us to do, but we don't see it or understand His will until we read His Word.

NOAH

Noah's father (Methusaleh) lived longer than anyone else in recorded history. Noah's grandfather was Enoch - a man who walked with God, so we see that Noah had a rich inheritance of faith from these men and he lived up to it well. From the time of creation, the hearts of men had worsened until they were *"only evil continually"* in Noah's day.

People were so bad that God was sorry He had created human beings and He was grieved. He decided to eliminate every living thing that He had made, BUT *"Noah found favor in the eyes of the Lord"*. There was one man who pleased God and God offered him an escape from the destruction that was to come.

God could have given Noah an ark, but instead He told Noah to build one and it took 120 years during which his neighbors ridiculed him day after day. It was difficult to explain why he would build a boat more than three football fields long when they were not near the ocean and it had never rained. What could he do with a boat in that dry place? Humanly speaking, Noah looked foolish, but he was obeying God because he believed what God had said. He told his neighbors what God had said, but they didn't believe Noah (or God) and continued in their sinful ways.

Noah foreshadows many things about Jesus - His favor in God's sight, His righteousness, His bloodline of believing forefathers and other things. He teaches us that God will provide an ark of safety for His people in the most severe of judgments. But there is a limit to what Noah can teach us for Jesus was the only begotten, holy Son of God. No one can fill His place as our Savior and Lord.

REMEMBER: "By faith Noah ... prepared an ark ... by which ... he became heir of the righteousness which is by faith" (Heb. 11:7).

NUMBERS

When the Children of Israel began their forty years of wandering in the wilderness, a census was taken. Another was taken when they ended that fruitless journey, and the Bible book called Numbers is named for this census-taking. They had lost the promises of God because of their unbelief and accusations against God. Their hearts were hard and rebellious, yet God proved His faithfulness even in the face of their resentment.

A year after their miraculous escape from Egypt, the Children of Israel waited while God gave Moses the Ten Commandments. Then, the census was taken by dividing the people into groups, three of which were the house of Jacob, the house of Joseph and the tribe of Levi who were to care for the tabernacle. After the count was made, they began their trek across the desert from Egypt to Israel following the cloud which hovered over the Ark of the Covenant. They marched in the order in which God had placed the tribes, each bearing the standard of their tribe. Dan was the last in line. They were last, but they were as much a part of the march as any other tribe.

Actually, being last was a place of strategic importance since there was danger of the Egyptians (or some other enemy) attacking from behind. We don't esteem last place, but someone has to occupy it and God values each of us equally. How like the world (and UNLIKE the Lord) it is to think that only those who come in first are important! People say, "Winning isn't the best thing - it's the ONLY thing!" but God never sees things that way. He says that the most important people are the ones who serve others. Are you "Number ONE"? Then, you're not the greatest among us - you may be the least! Read Luke 13:30.

REMEMBER: Jesus said, "Whosoever will be great among you, let him be be your minister (servant)."

OBADIAH

Although this name is hardly in popular use today, it carries a wonderful meaning - "servant of Jehovah". Several men of Scripture had this name, one of the most known was the prophet Obadiah. His prophecy had a great deal to do with what is today the land of Jordan. Unlike the countries to the east and west of it, Edom (as it was called then) has lots of water because of the mountains. Its capital city was Petra, a city carved out of solid red rock and protected by high cliffs. I have been there and have seen what remains to this day of the carvings and dwellings that once housed the Arabs of that day.

The Edomites were descendants of Esau and the hatred that existed between Easu and Jacob persisted down through the years between the Israelis and the Edomites until they were destroyed by Babylon in 582 B.C. We know little about Obadiah, but we know a lot about Edom and the times of which he wrote. The thing by which we remember them most is the fact that Edom refused to let Israel cross their land when they were in mortal danger, and when they were captured, Edom rejoiced.

God's attitude toward those who choose to be enemies of Israel was the same in those days as it is at the present - enemies of Israel are enemies of God Himself. Edom brought shame upon itself and God said that they *"would be cut off forever"* because they joined Israel's enemies to help capture those who escaped the army of Babylon. Today there is no such land as Edom nor a people known as Edomites. God's judgment was fulfilled and they suffered destruction. Their capital city is a ghost town visited by tourists as a forsaken place.

REMEMBER: God expects us to "love and comfort" Israel and He punishes those who stand against her. It was true then, and it is true today.

OIL

Our world has been drastically changed and greatly dominated by oil. We are so dependent on it for our way of life that we have sacrificed and suffered in order to gain and retain control of as much of the world's oil as possible. It has been used throughout human history, but never has it been more important than in our day. It is most useful in all its forms.

It has been used to seal ships and make them watertight since the days of Noah at least. It has been used in cooking, lighting, the treatment of disease and in the production of cosmetics. It has sealed buildings against the weather since the time of Daniel in Babylon and it is mentioned repeatedly in Scripture. It was used for anointing and for the lighting of the tabernacle and the temple. It was poured over the heads of those set apart to serve God and of men who were set apart to be king (Saul, David and Solomon). The ten virgins of Matthew 25 illustrate that it was used in their homes, and in the Old Testament, we are told that it was used in cooking and baking.

Most importantly, oil is used as a symbol of the Holy Spirit and each of its uses illustrates some function of the Holy Spirit in the life of the believer. He gives us light, protects against the storms of life, heals and beautifies us and is vital spiritual food that we need to sustain spiritual life and health. Moreover, He is a lubricant to keep the machinery of our lives functioning in good order without undue wear and tear like the oil in the engines of our cars. Like the oil in the cruse of the poor widow (II Kings 4), His supply is never exhausted nor depleted, but continually meets our needs beyond anything that we can explain.

REMEMBER: Jesus said that we are lights in the world and these lights are made to shine by the work of the Holy Spirit within us.

OLD

When we are asked how old we are, the manner in which we reply depends a great deal on what the answer is. A two-year-old proudly holds up two fingers and announces, "I'm two years old!" but a person who is fifty-two may be reluctant to reveal his true age. Then, by age eighty-two or ninety-two, we once again take pride in the stature that we have gained.

We use this word for expressing many things: the old ways (traditions), an old friend (intimacy), our old teacher (former things), old hat (overdone), the old man (disrespect), or we may say, "Oh! That old thing!" to show our disdain of an out-of-date item. In our country, we have a fetish for things that are new. Old things often are not valued as they are in other places. In the Bible, the Old Testament means that it is from the past and also that it is the former covenant that God held with men.

Scripture also used the term, "the old man", to refer to the sinful nature of man without Christ and contrasts this with "the new man" - a new creature in Christ Jesus. This new creation indicates that the life now being lived is the life of Christ within the individual and it is an eternal life with God. Christ makes this new life possible. He said, "I am ... the life, no man comes to the Father but by Me" (Jn. 14:6). Since Christ is life itself, without Him we are dead in sin and without hope - that's the "old man". Paul said, "Christ lives in me." That's the "new man" - the new life in Christ.

How about you? Are you "old" or "made new in Christ"? Today is the day to come to Christ and find life, abundant life. Whatever your age in years, life can begin anew in Christ Jesus.

REMEMBER: "Because of God's great love, even when we were dead in sins, made us alive together with Christ" (Eph. 2:5).

OMNIPOTENT

Although mentioned only once in the Bible, this word means "almighty" and is never used of anyone except God. Psalm 62 tells us that *"He rules by His power forever"*. How do we know this? Paul teaches us in Romans 1:20 that *"Since the creation of the world His invisible attributes, His eternal power and divine nature, have been clearly seen, **being understood through what has been made"**.* Nature teaches us about God's power.

We can consider the variety of things which God created - for instance, the grain of sand as compared to the stars of the sky, the snowflake which melts on our eyelash with the mountains which have endured, our breath on a frosty morning and a diamond which lies buried within a rock. Yet, in spite of the wide variety of things which God has created, we wonder if His power is actually limitless.

We must conclude that it is from His other attributes. God (by definition and by the teaching of Scripture) is infinite, the Bible calls Him such, but His infinity is not limited to space or time. Such limits are never mentioned. Then, it must follow that He cannot be limited in anything, not even in His power. Jesus said that His Father could do anything and went about demonstrating God's power by healing the sick and raising the dead while still making clear that our spiritual lives are of more importance to Him than our physical lives. Without His power, we have none, but God does not give His power away. What belongs to Him returns to Him. He remains omnipotent forever.

REMEMBER: God asked Job if he had "an arm like God?" or if he could "thunder with a voice like him? Deck thyself now with majesty and excellency," God said (Job 40:9-10). Then, God would agree that Job could save himself. But Job was helpless. Only *"the Lord God omnipotent reigneth"* (Rev. 19:6).

OMNISCIENT

Almost everyone has been called a "know-it-all" at some time or another. Of course, that term is used in sarcasm since no one knows everything except for God Himself. Humans are not omniscient and we need to learn. The motto of one school reads, "Let us learn on earth those things whose knowledge might continue in heaven." The philosopher Hegel wrote, "Peoples and governments never have learned from history, or acted on principles deduced from it." Thus, they have pointed out that the addition of knowledge to our thinking is not enough - we also need to gain wisdom, to really be able to use what we know.

"Shall any teach God knowledge?" (Job. 21:22) is an ancient question whose answer is obvious. Job 37 tells us that God is "perfect in knowledge" - omniscient. Dr. Tozer said that "God knows instantly and effortlessly all matter and all matters." That surely cannot be said of those of us who have labored over our school books, trying to learn enough to pass the next test!

Not only does God know all the laws of science, He also knows your thoughts and the innermost longings of your heart and mine. We can't fool Him, so why do we try? How much better to remember that He loves us infinitely and to come to Him with those things that concern us! God not only knows kings and world leaders, He also knows every child that is born ... and every tiny sparrow that flies and falls to the earth. He even knows the number of hairs on your head!

What troubles you today? Money? Health? Love? Sin? He knows about all of it and will rush to help you the moment you call on Him.

REMEMBER: Not only are God's power and His knowledge infinite - so is His love for you and me. Turn to Him today whatever your need.

PETER

It is possible today to visit the home of Peter's mother-in-law at the site of the city of Capernaum on the shore of the Sea of Galilee. It isn't hard to imagine the vociferous fisherman moving about, earning his living by fishing. There seems to be lots of space for this big man to have filled with his voice and his big frame. No doubt, he disturbed the peace of that tranquil seaside more than once with his boisterous lifestyle. His decision to follow Jesus was entered into with the same gusto that he did everything else. You never had to wonder about Peter!

When Jesus called him to become a "fisher of men", however, it meant that he could not run roughshod over others. God transformed him from a rough and tumble guy to a compassionate man who cared about those who were suffering. He offered them comfort and counsel by his letters. He had known hardship and God had met his need. Now, he could speak with authority ... and with gentleness ... about how a Christian is to accept and cope with suffering. For such discouraging times, Peter offers hope - *"a living hope by the resurrection of Jesus Christ from the dead"* (I Peter 1:3). Peter knew the discouragement of disappointment and the *"heaviness of many troubles"*, but he also knew that God's children are *"kept by the power of God through faith unto salvation"*. Peter knew for a certainty that *"the trial of our faith is much more precious than gold"* and that it will bring *"praise and honor and glory at the appearing of Jesus Christ"* (I Peter 1:5-7). Peter had experienced the fact that after we have suffered awhile, God *"will make us perfect, stablish, strengthen, settle us"*. Peter knew because it had already happened to him!

REMEMBER: Even Jesus had "to learn obedience by the things that He suffered"! God will use suffering in our lives to make us like Jesus.

PHILIPPIANS

The ancient city of Philippi still stands today in Greece even though it was founded nearly 400 years before Christ by Philip II, the father of Alexander. It was the site of a medical school - and a prison, as Paul found out! At the time of Paul's second missionary journey, a woman named Lydia lived there and carried on her business of selling purple dye much used in those days. She believed the things she heard Paul teach as did the jailer (and his family) who was responsible for Paul and Silas as they suffered in his prison there. After that time, Luke pastored the church there.

About six years later, Paul wrote to them and his letter indicates that it was a well established, thriving church. It was situated so far north that it actually constitutes the first European church, a notable penetration of the Gospel into Gentile territory. The household of Lydia became the focal point of the church - her family members and her servants forming the nucleus. Paul and his team had stayed with her when he was first there and the letter he wrote to Philippi is intimate and personal. He wrote to thank them for the money and clothes they had sent to him by way of Epaphroditus. No wonder Paul spoke of joy in this letter!

Because of the encouragement of such friends, Paul was thankful and joyful in the midst of trying circumstances. He exuded confidence in the Lord and in the strength that God gives to those who are faithful. He wrote of Christ's humility and obedience to His Father and urged the believers of Philippi to imitate such an attitude (Phil. 2). It was to these Christians that Paul revealed the longing of his heart to know Christ and to become more and more like Him.

REMEMBER: Believers are to encourage one another to do good works and to walk close to our beloved Savior.

POWER

It seems that one of the driving forces of mankind is the desire to gain and to hold power. We see it in sports, in business, in government and in family life. The Bible recognizes the importance of power by referring to it about 300 times.

Dr. E. R. Bertermann pointed out that "for many years, jutting rocks at Hell's Gate in New York Harbor proved a menace to shipping. They had to be removed, and they were blasted away with dynamite. Similar strength must remove every obstacle which would prevent us from believing Christ's resurrection with all our heart and soul. If we are to escape the terrors of the real Hell's Gate, every stone of doubt which still may stand before the Savior's grave must similarly be removed. For the safety of our souls ..., we must know *'the power of His resurrection.'*"

The Gospel of Jesus Christ is called *"the power of God unto salvation to everyone that believes"* by the Apostle Paul (Rom. 1:16). This "dynamite" is needed to break the bonds of sin and set the prisoners free. That power blasted Paul from his entrenched position as one who persecuted Christians to being the most vocal proponent of the faith that the world has ever known. It eventually cost him his life. Paul had seen the power of the Gospel at work to change the Roman world and challenge its leaders. Even the emperor was wary of Christians, driving them underground and feeding them to the lions. Yet even the most powerful ruler could not drive the faith of Jesus Christ from the hearts of the people, and eventually Constantine named Christianity the acknowledged church of the world.

REMEMBER: Satan is powerful, but Jesus Christ has all power. Like Paul, we can say, "The Gospel ... is the power of God unto salvation."

PRAYER

Although some people would make it mysterious, prayer is simply talking to God and listening for His voice. We are invited to come to God with our every concern, sharing it with Him openly and expecting Him to meet our needs in return. Jesus told us to *"ask, and it shall be given unto you"* (Luke 9). We are encouraged to come to God and are sure of finding a welcome.

Since God knows all things, however, we must be honest with Him as best we can for we cannot "pull the wool" over His eyes! We need to remember who He is when we speak to Him, too. After all, it is by His grace that we come - not because we have any inherent "right" to be there or to be heard by the Lord God Almighty. Yet, at the same time, the Holy Spirit Himself helps us to pray "as we ought" and Jesus makes intercession for us at the Throne of God's Grace.

We are to pray about everything - nothing is too large or too small, too important or too unimportant, too intimate or too grand to keep us from talking to our Heavenly Father about it. The lives we lead have an impact on our prayers, too. It isn't just whether or not we pray frequently, it is also imperative that we live righteously before God. He cares about the importance we place on spiritual matters and how much we conform to His image in our daily activities. Nonetheless, He hears our prayers based on His mercy and grace, not on our deeds.

We can pray for ourselves and for others with confidence that God will answer us according to His will. What joy there is in knowing that He will do what He wants to do about all the things we face in life.

REMEMBER: Prayer doesn't bring God down to us, it brings us up to Him! "Draw near to God, and He will draw near to you" (James 4:8).

PROPHECY

There is so much prophecy in the Bible that it is impossible to pass by this word. Someone has said that ninety per cent of Bible prophecy has been fulfilled and the other ten per cent remains to be fulfilled in the future. "Nobody knows the future," people often say. They're right - except for God. He not only knows the future, He has told us a great deal about it.

In the Old Testament, we read many things which have since become historical fact. These things have actually taken place just as they were predicted. Daniel wrote of the great empires of the world and in the intervening centuries, these empires have risen and fallen one after the other in exactly the manner described in Scripture. Daniel's prophecies were so precise that some have tried to say that his book was written AFTER those things had occurred instead of many centuries beforehand when Daniel lived! A careful study of language, however, shows that Daniel wrote in a manner used in his own day and not as the language came to be used later. The old style was lost for many years and this fact only came to light in succeeding centuries - too late for such a farce to have been carried out.

Why, then, are some surprised that believers expect to hear from God as they seek to live for Him? God tells us many things on a personal level, yet God's leading in our lives must never conflict with Scripture as God has already given it to us, nor will He reveal any new revelation beyond the pages of the Bible. Anyone who claims to have a new revelation of truth from God is not to be trusted for God's Word itself warns us against adding to what we have received. God will not contradict Himself!

REMEMBER: What we need is not new revelation of truth, but obedience to the truth of God which has already been revealed to us.

PROVERBS

In this practical book of the Bible, we find many short sayings which tell us wisdom. More than a book of facts, we find here the way to put information to good use in our lives. If we live by this book, we will find "words to live by" in every circumstance of life.

Contrary to our modern era, the search for information is not as highly rated as is the pursuit of wisdom. The first nine chapters of Proverbs stresses the importance of wisdom and its value in our lives. Its opposite, folly, is revealed as the treasure of fools which leads them along a path of destruction. Solomon, the wisest man who ever lived, shares with us many bits of wisdom which enhanced his life, closing with praise for "the virtuous woman" for which he used his mother, Bathsheba, as his model.

Here we learn that *"a good name is rather to be chosen than great riches, and loving favor rather than silver and gold."* Memorizing this verse at the encouragement given me by my mother has stood me in good stead in all the intervening years. Then she followed her admonition by giving us a good name to treasure and protect.

She also pointed out that *"a soft answer turneth away wrath; but grievous words stir up anger"* (Prov. 15:1). Knowing this influenced my actions when I was seated on a plane flying south from Pittsburgh near two men who were using Jesus' name blasphemously. I was offended, so I handed them a tract saying, "I heard you talking about Christ. This will tell you more about Him." I heard no more swearing from them that day.

REMEMBER: "The fear of the Lord is the beginning of wisdom, And the knowledge of the Holy One is understanding" (Prov. 9:10).

PSALMS

Psalms are simply songs "fit to be sung, whether they be historical, doctrinal, prayer or praise." We learn from them while we are praising God and worshipping Him. Paul said, *"Let the word of Christ dwell in you richly in all wisdom; teaching and admonishing one another in psalms and hymns and spiritual songs, singing with grace in your hearts to the Lord"* (Col. 3:16). A singer needs to know God's word so he (or she) can be sure they are conveying God's truth and wisdom, not just prattling on about some unimportant matter.

Jesus said that the psalms "spoke" of Him and He equated them in truth with the books of Moses and the writings of the prophets. Matthew Henry, that great scholar of the Bible, wrote that the Psalms are "one of the choicest parts of all the Old Testament; so much is in it of Christ and His gospel, as well as of God and His law, that it has been called the summary of both Testaments." It is truly a book of inspiration and worship to our God.

Here we find the contrast between the righteous and the wicked and the resulting happiness or destruction. God's Word and its exalted place in our lives is presented at length and in terms so clear that we teach small children these verses before they are hardly old enough to know the words their tender lips utter. Let us join David in revelling in God's Word.

Henry Halley wrote, "Trust is the foremost idea in all the book. Whatever the occasion, joyous or terrifying, it drove David straight to God. Whatever his weaknesses, David literally lived in God. Praise was always on his lips."

REMEMBER: Although David often spoke of the justice, righteousness and wrath of God, His mercy was the thing in which David gloried.

QUAKE

Earthquakes are as terrifying as anything the human race experiences. When the earth quakes, people quiver with dread and panic because of the fear that strikes hearts when our usually solid foundation (the earth) shakes beneath our feet and causes our homes and other buildings to move on their foundations.

This word appears in the Bible eight times in its various forms. The first is part of the account concerning Moses and the tables of the law which God gave at Mount Sinai. God met Moses on that barren mountain to give him His laws, and when He came to earth in that place, the earth shook ... and so did Moses! Moses said, *"I exceedingly fear and quake!"* (Heb. 12:11). When the law was ended at the death of Christ, the earth shook again. *"Jesus, when He had cried again with a loud voice, yielded up the ghost.... The veil of the temple was rent ... and the earth did quake"* (Matt. 27:50,51). The earth shook when *"the angel of the Lord descended from heaven"* (Matt. 28:2) to let the disciples into the empty tomb. The earth will shake again when Jesus returns to set up His kingdom on earth.

Frequent earthquakes are a sign of the approaching return of Christ. Does that ring a bell with you? There have been literally thousands of earthquakes in the news in recent months - more than ever before.

"God has promised, saying, Yet once more I shake not the earth only, but also heaven ... that those things which are shaken ... will be removed so that those things which cannot be shaken may remain" (Heb. 27:28).

REMEMBER: The only safe place to stand is on Christ the Solid Rock - "all other ground is sinking sand".

QUENCH

When Isaiah wrote of the gentleness of Jesus, he said that He would not break "a bruised reed" nor quench "the smoking flax". This is a beautiful picture of how Jesus preserves and restores those things which are on their last legs, so to speak. Broken, hurt, discouraged people will be restored and rebuilt by a loving Savior - they will not be quenched (Isa. 42, Matt. 12).

So often, well meaning people do terrible harm to those they try to help. Gifts to a ne'er-do-well make him lazier. Rescuing a wayward child only makes him expect more help the next time he gets into trouble. Gentle, tender people are often misguided in their endeavors to help others, and some offer help in order to make themselves feel good! Too often, "we thrust our calloused hands among the heartstrings of a friend," but not Jesus. His scarred hands are always tender, and He knows us so well that He helps us without hurting us at the same time. Jesus healed everyone who came to Him - even when that meant staying with the people for hours and hours, until He was exhausted.

Ephesians six is a challenging message for believers and we are told to *"take the shield of faith, wherewith we shall be able to quench all the fiery darts of the wicked"* (Eph. 6:16). When under attack, we are to put our faith to work and by faith put out all the fires of doubt the devil sends our way.

Paul used this word when writing to the Thessalonians, too. He warned them not to quench the Spirit of God in their lives. We can be so distracted by life and its problems that we actually extinguish His work in us. We are warned not to let this happen, yet we see many believers whose eyes are dull and their hearts heavy for lack of the work of the Holy Spirit.

REMEMBER: The Holy Spirit has been sent to be our Comforter and Encourager. Don't push Him out of your life!

QUESTIONS

In Hebrew and Greek there are several shades of meaning for this everyday word, but we can best understand it by the ways in which it is used.

Even at the age of twelve, Jesus was asking ... and answering questions. Even His family was surprised that He discussed the weighty matters of the Law with the most learned men of His day when He went to the Temple. Those theologians had never seen a boy like Jesus who could carry on a deep discussion of the tenets of their faith. Yet, Jesus would respond to the simplest questions of His fishermen friends or those of the children who loved Him so much (Luke 2:41-52).

One question of the disciples was answered with the Lord's Prayer for they simply asked Jesus how they should pray. He answered, *"Our Father which is in heaven, hallowed by Thy Name ...."* Another question was, *"How should we live?"* Jesus' answer is called, "The Beatitudes" where He describes the virtues of humility and sorrow as they work in the lives of believers.

God never turns away the questions of an honest doubter. He welcomes them as Jesus welcomed the questions that lurked in the heart of Thomas. We are not to hide our questions away in guilt for even asking them, or in embarrassment that we don't understand already. Jesus invites us to ask so that we may receive answers for our uncertain hearts. One man asked the most important question of all when he said, "What must I do to be saved?" Have you asked that question? Have you found the answer? Paul said, *"Believe on the Lord Jesus Christ and you will be saved" (Acts 16:30-31).* That's the promise of God!

REMEMBER: Jesus stands waiting for our questions, but He won't enter our hearts and our homes until we invite Him to come in.

QUIET

A family of four went out into the chilly night, each one armed with a snow shovel. In spite of the scraping sounds of their shovels, the serenity of the night was undisturbed. Peace settled into their hearts as they cleared away the snow from the storm that had passed and prepared the driveway and sidewalks for the next day. The night was quiet all right, but there was a quiet in their hearts and minds that was much more profound. Often, the only quiet the human heart can find is the calm that comes from holding fast to our faith in spite of the clamor of life.

Quietness in the land is important to God so that His Word can flourish and reach out in peace to the needy hearts of our world. When there is famine or war, popularity or tragedy, our lives are shattered and there is no place to rest in tranquility and consider the things of God.

We're told that the decibels of noise in the ghetto areas of our major cities are many times higher than the noise level in the suburbs. The weariness brought on by this constant battle against noise accounts for some of the restlessness and trouble that are so common there as well. People need rest ... they need to be quiet and find the peace that comes from knowing our sins are forgiven. *"There is no peace, saith the Lord, unto the wicked"* (Isa. 48:22).

Perhaps you haven't thought about personal peace very much. The Psalmist spoke of it a great deal and his advice was, *"Seek peace, and pursue it."* God promises to keep those of us *"in perfect peace, whose minds are stayed on Thee,"* because we trust in Him (Isa. 26:3).

REMEMBER: We can rest when we remember that God is in control of all things and no one can prevent Him from keeping His promises.

RAPTURE

This word is often used by believers; however, it is never found on the pages of Scripture. Instead, Paul wrote of this event, saying, *"The Lord himself shall descend from heaven with a shout ... and the dead in Christ shall rise first; then we who are alive and remain shall be caught up together with them ... to meet the Lord in the air"* (I Thess. 4:16-17).

His coming is pictured in the marriage traditions of the Jewish wedding. An engaged couple remain in their respective homes for at least a year before the wedding while the groom prepares their new home. Meanwhile, the bride (not knowing exactly when he will come) must stay in a state of readiness. When everything is ready for his bride, the groom and his friends go to her home to steal her away. She and her friends listen for their coming and she dons her wedding dress and is ready to go with him when he comes. The happy group leaves her parents' home and goes to the place he has prepared where the wedding takes place with a wedding feast that goes on for seven days.

This attitude of preparedness was reflected by a little girl who tidied her room each morning so that she would be ready if Jesus were to come on that day. Believers must be ready, too, for Jesus will come with no warning to take us to His heavenly home... and ours! Then, we will be with Him forevermore. No more tears. No more crying. No more sadness. Only joy in His presence forever! No wonder we use a word for His coming that indicates feelings that are beyond description. Fanny Crosby wrote a hymn with these words: "Blessed are those whom the Lord finds watching, In His glory they shall share; If He shall come at the dawn or midnight, Will He find us watching there?"

REMEMBER: Let's make this our daily prayer, "Even so, come, Lord Jesus."

REDEMPTION

This word pictures bondage and powerlessness, and the price that is paid to release the prisoner. Years ago, we saved "green stamps" with our purchases and many of the little extras in our homes were secured when we went to the "redemption center" with our books of stamps. There we purchased the coveted item with our books of stamps. The stamps were effective to buy what we wanted when we presented them at the redemption store.

In Africa, tribal chiefs whose people were being taken by slave traders could buy back those they held most dear ... if they could pay the price. Just so, the sinner is redeemed from the bondage of his sin when God presents the blood of His Son on our behalf. He comes to the "store" where the sinner is held in the power of sin and offers the evidence of His right to redeem us by the blood of the Lamb of God and calls our name. We then belong to Him by virtue of the fact that He has redeemed us. *"Know ye not that ... you are not your own? You are bought with a price; therefore, glorify God in your body and in your spirit, which are God's"* (I Cor. 6:19-20).

There is no hesitation on God's part to claim us as His own, and with that go certain obligations on our part. We are no longer "the captain of our fate", we have been redeemed and now we have a responsibility to glorify God with our actions and our attitudes in life. What a privilege to represent a loving God in this wicked, wayward world and show others the goodness of our God. How gracious our God who gives us His name to carry with us wherever we go. We are the picture of His grace, mercy and love to everyone we meet. Jesus said, *"Whosoever commits sin is the servant of sin,"* but now we are redeemed!

REMEMBER: "The wages of sin is death, but the gift of God is eternal life through Jesus Christ our Lord" (Rom. 6:23).

REFUGE

The world is a dangerous place - I'm sure you've already noticed that. There aren't many places we can go for refuge, either, since most people are interested in themselves above all others. Mothers are known for their selflessness and there are those outstanding people like Mother Theresa and organizations like the Red Cross which exist to help people. These people stand out because of their service to humanity. No wonder people through the ages have found refuge in God's Word.

In Old Testament days (the Book of Numbers), God commanded the Children of Israel to set aside six cities as places of refuge where a man could go if he had killed someone by accident. Once there, he was safe - protected from the revenge that others might seek for the death of their loved one.

This picture of safety and retreat is carried over to a spiritual sense for our souls can find refuge in no one except God from the world and its trials and tribulations, from the devil and his temptations, and from the weakness we find in our own selves. God is a stronghold in which we can hide "until the storms of life are over", as the old hymn states. Jesus invited us to come to Him and find rest from our trials and the battles we fight within and from outside ourselves (Matt. 11:25).

There is refuge in God ... and we need protection from many things, but how do we find it? Jesus said, *"I am the way, the truth and the life; no man comes to the Father, but by me"* (Jn. 14:6). If we are to enter the safety of our heavenly refuge, we must first come to Jesus, acknowledge Him as God's Son and the sacrifice for our sins. By Him, we have access to all the benefits of the Heavenly Father.

REMEMBER: Jesus also said, "Him that comes to me, I will not cast out."

REIGN

Royalty! How we are fascinated by those privileged ones who live the kind of fairy tale we sometimes dream about. Yet, human royalty often falls short of the bliss and glory we like to think belongs to them. More often, such lives are cursed by too much attention and wealth, and too little purpose and goals for their existence. The very things that we think would be wonderful to have (like wealth and fame) often turn into life-destroying "assets".

God's reign over all comes from the fact that He created everything. No wonder the unbeliever tries to deny God's creative work! He is unwilling to accept God's reign in his heart and life and he seeks any means available to throw off God's claim. Rebellion against God is recorded throughout the Bible.

One story of such rebellion is found in Joseph where his brothers hated the dream God sent Joseph telling of his dominion over them, but in time, Joseph held the answer to their famine and they did, indeed, bow down to him. Jospeh's love for them and the forgiveness he offered them is a wonderful picture of God's attitude toward us - loving, forgiving, caring for us even though we have rebelled against Him.

Moses said (after he and his people had been delivered from Egypt), *"The Lord shall reign for ever and ever"* (Ex. 15:18). This truth is echoed and re-echoed in the New Testament from the prophecy of Jesus' birth (*"He shall reign over the house of Jacob forever"* - Lk. 1:33) to Revelation when His glorious second coming is foretold. This world's kingdoms come under the rule of Christ in spite of their disdain, *"and He shall reign for ever and ever"* (Rev. 11:15). Every knee will bow before Jesus.

REMEMBER: We can acknowledge Him as Lord today, or we will be required to bow before Him in the day of judgment.

RELIGION

A religion is a system of faith and worship, but no man-made system can be pure or undefiled, so because of the flaws we see, we are often discouraged and disillusioned by religion instead of finding God by means of it. No one is ever saved by religion (mentioned 7 times in the Bible) for it is not acts of devoted worship which redeem our souls, but the blood of Jesus Christ in His death on the cross which provides redemption.

Nonetheless, the Bible tells us that *"Pure religion and undefiled ... is this: to visit the fatherless and widows in their affliction, and to keep oneself unspotted from the world"* (James 1:27). Some who appear to be religious (or who claim to be religious) seem unable to speak kindly of others. Such religious claims and pretenses are ineffective and do not constitute real faith in God. Jesus said that those who love Him will keep His commandments - the first one is to love God and others.

So Christianity (in the truest sense) is not a religion at all. Religious leaders die - we know where they are buried - but Jesus rose from the dead. His tomb is empty. Religions continue on without their leaders, but Christianity cannot be separated from Jesus Christ - knowing Him, believing Him and seeking to follow Him daily. Religions devised by men require that people do something to earn the right to be with God ... or to be a god. Not so with Christianity! Here God has done something for us which we could not do for ourselves. He has redeemed us - paid the price for our sin when we were lost and helpless - and He freely offers salvation to anyone who asks Him for it. Faith in Christ means admitting that we are not good, nor can we be - but He is! He offers His goodness to us from the storehouse of His love.

REMEMBER: Religion cannot save us. Jesus said, "I am come to seek and to save that which was lost" (Lk. 19:10).

REST

Sometimes we equate rest with sleep, but as many people have learned, it is possible to rest without sleeping and/or sleep without resting. The insomniac who can lie quietly at ease can rest while the person who sleeps fitfully can wake unrefreshed - weary from the effort of sleeping. Beyond that there is the rest of the mind and soul which is just as needed as rest for our bodies.

Even God rested when He had finished His creation work, and He surely intends that we rest, too. When we come to a place of trust and reliance upon God and His love for us, we find the kind of repose that strengthens us for the trials of life. We call that "resting in the Lord" and it is much harder to find than sleep. Still, we can rest in God by trusting in Christ minute by minute.

Believing that God has a plan for all things (including us and our lives) can bring us to a place where we know that *"all things work together for good to them that love God"*. He loves us more than we can understand. His power is such that He can do whatever He wants to do - and He wants to show us His goodness! The stress of life is not beyond His care and keeping - He can handle it. When we're overwhelmed and exhausted, He has more than enough strength and energy to do whatever needs to be done. God is on our side!

So much of life is beyond our control. We all arrive at a day and a point at which we do not decide the outcome of things. So much is taken out of our hands, but no one can take over control from God. "He's got the whole world in His hands" is not just a nice saying - it's true!

REMEMBER: Jesus said, "Come unto Me, and I will give you rest. Take My yoke upon you ... and you shall find rest unto your souls" (Matt. 11:28).

RESURRECTION

Lord Salisbury was a well known British statesman and scientist. He was also a man of great faith. He claimed that the resurrection was the central point of his faith. He believed it:

"First, because it was testified to by men who had every opportunity of seeing and knowing, and whose veracity was tested by the most tremendous trials both of energy and endurance during long lives; and secondly, because of the remarkable effects it had upon the world."

Many people had opportunity to see Jesus after He was resurrected from the dead - far too many to keep a false story straight. Cephas and the twelve disciples saw Jesus. They had opportunity to talk to Him, touch Him and decide for themselves if He was some sort of apparition or if He was truly alive again. Five hundred "brethren" saw Him, too. James saw Him and "all of the apostles" which seems to refer to those who claimed to be His followers. These all saw so much that they knew this Jesus was resurrected for He entered closed rooms without using the locked door, and He did many other signs which are not recorded for us (Jn. 20:30) because it was as hard for the disciples to believe He died and rose again as it would be for us.

We have to take their word for Christ's resurrection - and God's word for it since He teaches us to believe that Christ was raised from the dead so that it might no longer have power over us. We now find refuge from the power of death because of Jesus' resurrection! God has written the promise of resurrection into His Word ... and also into every leaf of springtime.

REMEMBER: "If you confess ... the Lord Jesus, and shall believe ... that God has raised Him from the dead, you will be saved" (Rom. 10:9).

REVELATION

When we consider who we are and who God is, we should be amazed that He bothers to explain things to us at all, yet He has gone to great lengths to reveal His plan and program in His Word. The Old Testament tells us that God would send someone who would do marvelous things. The New Testament tells us who He is and what He did, but it also goes on to tell us what He will do in the future. The last book of the Bible is "The Revelation of Jesus Christ" even though many people just call it "Revelations". It isn't just random revelations - it is THE Revelation of Jesus as we will see Him when He comes to rule and to reign upon the earth. We read there a description of the glory that will be Christ's when He comes in great power. It is more than we can understand - we have never seen anything like it. Yet, He repeats His usual invitation to us to open the door of our hearts and let Him in so He can fellowship with us.

The New Jerusalem is more glorious than anything we have ever seen, too. There is no such city on this earth, nor will there be until Christ's coming. After the great and terrible judgment on those who refuse Him, we see magnificent glory which dazzles our eyes and power to destroy His enemies and build His own kingdom that we cannot comprehend. Yet, we are told to expect all these things at His coming - and much more! We have wonderful hope for the future when we look at Christ and His plans for the time that yet shall be upon the earth.

If we feel deprived in this lifetime, let's look ahead to the riches of His coming. If we have been treated unjustly, let's remember that He will rule in righteousness and truth.

REMEMBER: "We, according to His promise, look for new heavens and a new earth, in which dwells righteousness" (I Peter 3:13).

REVEREND

According to the Bible, this word can only refer to God. *"He sent redemption unto His people; He has commanded His covenant forever; holy and reverend is His name"* (Ps. 111:9). Just as none of us is holy except for the holiness which God gives us, so none of us is reverend ("terrible"). God is so great and mighty that we will be overwhelmed when we see Him in His glory.

Do you remember the disciples who stood with Christ when He was transfigured on the mountain top? They fell at His feet completely awestruck for they had never seen anyone or anything that could compare with His greatness.

We are to honor those who serve the Lord as His ministers - this is clearly taught in the New Testament. *"Know them who labor among you, and are over you in the Lord, and admonish you ... esteem them very highly in love for their work's sake"* (II Thess. 5:12-13). Nevertheless, this respect does not approach the reverence that we are to give to our God. Only He is "holy and reverend". Ministers are mortal men who have dedicated their lives to the service of the King of kings; however, we are not to confuse them with the King himself.

Jesus said His ministers were not to be called "master" or "father", but the highest title was to be called "servants of the Most High God" (Matt. 23:8-11). We are all brothers in Jesus Christ. None of us is master of the other. Only Christ is our Master. We have only one Father, and He is in heaven. Jesus said, "He that is greatest among you shall be your servant. He that shall humble himself shall be exalted" (Matt. 23:11-12).

REMEMBER: "Thou art worthy, O Lord, to receive glory and honor and power; for thou hast created all things" (Rev. 4:11).

ROMANS

On a jet from Manila to Singapore, I sat by the window while a medical doctor sat next to the aisle. The seat between us was empty. When he learned I was a minister, he leaned toward me and asked, "Is salvation by faith alone, or is it by good works?" How clearly the Bible answers this question!

"Not by works of righteousness which we have done, but according to His mercy He saved us, by the washing of regeneration, and renewing of the Holy Spirit" (Titus 3:5).

We were *"dead in trespasses and sins"*, as helpless to do good works as a corpse in the morgue. There was nothing we could do about our sins ... or anything else! God took pity on us and did for us what we could not do for ourselves—that which we did not deserve! His *"great mercy"* and His love moved Him to save us from our sin - He washed us and poured the oil of His Holy Spirit on us, making us new creatures filled with His life.

My doctor friend on the airplane had been reading the Bible and he found it to be different from what he'd heard before. The differences made him curious and he asked that simple question. The answer made him want to trust in Christ for his salvation instead of spending his life trying to be good enough for heaven.

"For by grace are you saved through faith; and that not of yourselves, it is the gift of God - not of works, lest any man should boast. For we are His workmanship, created in Christ Jesus unto good works, which God has before ordained that we should walk in them" (Eph. 2:8-10).

REMEMBER: Good works are done by grateful people whose sins have been washed in the blood of the Lamb!

ROME

In Jesus' day, Rome was the capital of the world. Roman armies had conquered most of the countries of the world and their crushing domination was inescapable. Their culture, however, lacked the vitality to take over the minds of men, so Greek language and culture remained in place. Still, the reins of government were in the hands of the Romans without question. The seeds of the Christian faith were carried to Rome as they spread to all the world in those early days of the church. Paul wanted to visit those believers just as he had so many others and he wrote to them from Corinth at the time of Nero's reign.

Paul wrote about the grace of God - how He offers to those who are unworthy the complete salvation purchased by Jesus' blood when He died on the Cross. He describes in detail the helplessness of mankind when faced with the power of sin - how only God can deliver us from it and make us fit to be called God's children. Paul also spent time to mark the difference between trying to keep the Mosaic Law and accepting God's free gift of salvation. He outlines for the church at Rome (and for us) the teaching of God concerning judgment of sin and the rewards of faith in Jesus. Paul explains patiently the distinctives of the new nature given to believers as opposed to the characteristics of the old nature. He also wrote something of himself and his spiritual relationship with God and His Son Jesus Christ. *"I am crucified with Christ ... I am not ashamed of the gospel of Christ ... The wrath of God is revealed from heaven against all ungodliness ... All have sinned ... The gift of God is eternal life through Jesus Christ our Lord."* What glorious phrases flowed from the heart of Paul when he wrote to the Romans!

REMEMBER: "Believe on the Lord Jesus Christ and you will be saved."

RUTH

Ruth grew up in the land of Moab - a land not blessed by God as was the Land of Israel. Still, she was selected by a Jewish man to be his wife when his family moved there to escape a famine. Even God's Chosen People are not without times of trouble! In time, all the men of Naomi's family died, leaving the women to fend for themselves. Naomi could think only of going home. So gracious was their relationship that her two daughters-in-law decided to go with her, but only Ruth went all the way. Ruth's declaration of loyalty stands today as a beautiful pledge of love suitable for use in today's Christian weddings.

"Entreat me not to leave thee, or to return from following after thee, for whither thou goest I will go and where thou lodgest I will lodge. Thy people will be my people, and thy God my God" (Ruth 1:16).

Ruth's love extended beyond her mother-in-law to the God whom she served, and Ruth's faith was put to the test when she went to the fields to gather grain to feed herself and Naomi. Her beauty did not escape notice, however, and Naomi recognized special generosity in the "leftovers" she took home. Naomi also recognized that the giver was her relative! So, Naomi instructed Ruth in the law of the Kinsman Redeemer. A man in the family of a widow could take her as his wife, and Boaz claimed this right and proposed marriage to Ruth after he redeemed her from a relative who had a nearer relationship. Just so, we have been redeemed from our spiritual poverty and hopelessness, but *"We were not redeemed with corruptible things such as silver and gold, but with the precious blood of Christ."*

REMEMBER: Before Ruth met Boaz, she and Naomi were poor and hopeless. That's how we all are until we meet Jesus Christ.

SALT

What we need for salt is not a definition, but a taste! Its uses and purposes are most significant, however, for salt is most useful in everyday life. What we expect from salt is not its own flavor, but the flavor of other foods enhanced by salt. What we get from salt is not its own preservation, but the preserving qualities it provides for other foods. We don't ask that salt be palatable, but that it make a thousand other foods palatable.

We use expressions like "take it with a grain of salt" and "they are the salt of the earth" to convey disdain or value in commonplace terms. In soup, salt permeates the whole and makes it better. Yet, if salt loses its flavor, it is worthless and good for nothing but paving material, and its flavor can be lost by resting near common dirt. Jesus said that His followers are to be the salt of the earth, changing the "flavor" of life around us, but if we become part of the world, we lose our ability to make a difference in the lives of people - we become worthless.

Bishop Pickett said, "Men have tried to flavor life with the salts of this world. The result is that life becomes boring and pointless. Disillusionment shadows all because men do not have that in their hearts which will flavor life with purpose, meaning and happiness." Jesus said that He came to give us life, abundant life ... flavorful life, if you will. Our only ability to do that for others is by means of His life within us. The words Jesus spoke, the truths He taught are the only things we have to share with desperate, hopeless people. Only Christ can give the kind of life that has meaning and purpose.

REMEMBER: Salt is a common, inexpensive item found in every kitchen and used daily by everyone in one form or another. Christians are to be like that - everywhere and useful!

SECURE

It seems today that those who speak and write for the public have set out to frighten everyone out of their wits! I don't just mean the scary, horror movies and television. I mean the newscasters and editorial writers who drum away on the dangers of modern existence. Their specials include such things as "Radon in your home", "Lead in your drinking water" and a thousand other warnings to which we are supposed to give attention. How can anyone find peace of mind?

No one can deny that life has its rough times. We'd be foolish to try to convince anyone over the age of ten that life is a bed of roses! As believers there is a confidence which can keep us steady in the most trying of circumstances—God is in control! His power is not diminished. His love for us has not waned. His plan for our salvation has not changed. Today's problems are temporary—His love and care are eternal, unchanging, they will not fade away. *"He that has begun a good work in you will perform it until the day of Jesus Christ"* (Phil 1:6).

We can depend on God, His plan and His love for us. Yet, we must not become complacent in this assurance - we're not to take God for granted. Just as we are not pleased when others take us for granted, so God wants us to think of Him and remember that it is from His hand that our blessings come. So often, when trouble is at low tide, so is our devotion to God. Many times we call on Him the most when we feel the need of Him most - when we're in trouble! He wants us to turn to Him, so He sends us problems to drive us back to His side. Why should we be surprised by this? Our relationship to Him is what He values most. He will teach us by our suffering. He will discipline us.

REMEMBER: Whom the Lord loves, He corrects just as a father corrects the son who is his delight.

SIN

Today's speech patterns often include what have become known as "four-letter words". The Bible, however, uses a three-letter word which most foul-mouthed people seldom use—sin. Nearly 600 times, this word appears in Scripture. In fact, it can be said that the Bible is all about sin and forgiveness.

Adam and Eve were created perfect—sinless and innocent. Yet, they brought sin into the human race when they were tempted by the devil who had been one of God's chief angels. Lucifer's pride and his greedy desire to be "higher" than God Himself caused his downfall, but he did not fall alone. One third of the angels followed him in his rebellion against God. The Bible describes sin as a disease like leprosy, a condition like slavery, an attitude equivalent to murder. Even the "smallest sin" is a drastic contradiction against God and His holiness ... and we are all sinners!

It has been said, "Sin is a clenched fist, and its object is the face of God!" Again, "Sin offers itself as a friend, then becomes a fiend!" What can we do about sin? It creeps silently into our lives and leads us where we do not want to go, yet we seem powerless to drive it away. That's why God's truth is so wonderful! It deals with sin, breaks its power in our lives, and ultimately destroys it altogether.

We are infected with the leprosy of sin, yet the Great Physician heals us making our hearts as pure and white as newfallen snow. We are captured as slaves in the marketplace of sin, yet the Redeemer purchases our souls from the bondage we have known and sets us free to live for Him.

REMEMBER: Psalm 119:11 says, "Thy word have I hid in my heart that I might not sin against Thee." God's Word will keep us from sin.

SOLOMON

This king lived about 1,000 years before Christ was born in Bethlehem. He was the second son of David and Bathsheba and was reared with every advantage a child could have. Although not next in line for his father's throne, Solomon came to power after a failed coup by one of his half-brothers. His grandfather had been one of David's chief advisors.

In spite of all of this, Solomon sought wisdom from the Lord. He knew that true understanding and discernment come only from God. His choice was so pleasing to God that He also gave him great riches and honor throughout the world and down through history. His wisdom has been set down for us in the Book of Proverbs - a treasury of information on how to live from day to day. He also wrote Song of Solomon and Ecclesiastes where Solomon wrote respectively of youth and age.

Early in his life, Solomon was promised his father's throne. His brothers conspired to take the throne when David was old, but Bathsheba's reminder was all that it took for David to appoint Solomon to the throne. David also charged him with the building of the temple since God had not allowed David to build it. His role as warrior caused God to seek a man of peace to build His house of worship. So, Solomon came to power with his father's blessing, the approval of his people and the commission of God upon him to build the temple. He had everything that life could give, yet his later years were marred by disillusionment and weariness of heart. Solomon had too much of this life. His wisdom did not feed his heart and soul unless he walked with God, that great Fountain of all that is wise and good.

REMEMBER: It is not wisdom, fame or glory that give life meaning. Our hearts find rest as we "Fear God, and keep His commandments" (Ecc. 12:13).

SOUL

In the scientific era, there were those who chose to deny the soul of man since it is impossible to define, measure, or evaluate scientifically. One such scientist challenged a minister saying that man was made up of a few chemicals worth only a few cents. The scientist scoffed when he refused the challenge saying, "How can a reasonable man say that I have a soul?" The minister said, "Why should I discuss such things with something that is no more than a collection of chemicals worth only a few cents? These things do not have intelligence. I don't care to discuss this with one who has no intelligence." Obviously, that ended the discussion for man has intelligence ... and he also has a soul.

Scripture uses the word "soul" more than 500 times in such a way as to indicate that a soul is immaterial, dwelling within the body. A soul without a body is incomplete. It has identifiable attributes which are expressed by emotions. Without doubt, the Bible also teaches that the soul has a future existence beyond the portals of death.

Jesus spoke often about man's soul. *"Fear not them which kill the body, but are not able to kill the soul"* (Matt. 10:28). *"What shall it profit a man, if he gain the whole world and lose his own soul?"* (Mk. 8:36). We also need to remember that *"man became a living soul"* when God breathed the breath of life into Adam who had been formed from the dust of the earth. He was only a lump of clay until God breathed life into him. Even more, our lives resemble lumps of clay until God breathes spiritual life into them and makes us truly "alive" unto God and dead to sin. This is a beautiful picture of what happens when we let God's Holy Spirit permeate our souls with His life.

REMEMBER: We can only say that all is well with our souls when God has given us His life by faith in Jesus Christ.

SPIRIT

Many times, this word is used interchangeably with "soul", but there is a distinction to be made here for Scripture uses both words to indicate that the human being is made up of spirit, soul and body. Perhaps we can best understand the difference by looking at Adam and Eve in the Garden of Eden. There they fellowshipped with God, experiencing all the emotions and consciousness that we experience in life. The relationship between soul and spirit did not immediately become apparent. However, when Eve took of the forbidden fruit of the tree, God said she would die. The serpent said, "You shall not surely die!" Eve's body did not die when she sinned, yet, we cannot believe that God was mistaken! The question becomes, "What died when Eve sinned against God?" Her soul did not die for she still loved Adam and experienced emotions. It was her spirit that died. Her connection with God was broken when she sinned.

Job wrote long ago that *"There is a spirit in man, and the inspiration of the Almighty giveth him understanding."* It is with our spirits that we understand God, love Him and worship Him. The first thing that happened to Adam and Eve was that they became conscious of themselves and their nakedness, and they made aprons of fig leaves to cover themselves. Prior to their sin, they had only been conscious of God. The Psalmist indicated that his redemption was that of his spirit - "Into thine hand I commit my spirit; thou hast redeemed me, God of truth" (Ps. 31:5). Solomon wrote, "The spirit of man is the candle of the Lord" (Prov. 20:27), and "The dust shall return to the earth as it was: and the spirit shall return unto God who gave it" (Eccles. 12:7). When capitalized, Spirit refers to the Holy Spirit of God, third person of the Trinity.

REMEMBER: "God is a spirit, and they that worship Him must worship Him in spirit and in truth" (Jn. 4:24).

STAR

How exciting have been the recent discoveries made about the stars and planets by means of the Hubble Telescope and other studies. Scientists have been able to measure the rate of expansion of the universe and to find its outer limits. This shows that the universe is not limitless, but defined in size even though it is expanding. Moses clearly stated that God made the stars (Gen. 1:16). The Psalmist wrote, *"When I consider Your heavens, the work of Your fingers, The moon and the stars, which You have ordained ...."* They had no doubt about where the stars of heaven had come from. The Psalmist also declared that God had named them (Ps. 147:4), and some of their names are used in Scripture (Job 9:9, 38:31, Amos 5:8). David said that the *"heavens declare the glory of God"* (Ps. 19:1).

God made a great distinction, however, stating that we should not worship the bodies of the heavens. Deuteronomy 4:19 says to beware *"lest thou lift up thine eyes unto heaven and when thou seest the sun and the moon and the stars, even all the host of heaven, and shouldst be driven to worship, and serve them which the Lord thy God hath divided unto all nations under the whole heaven."* We are not to worship the creation, but the Creator.

Recent discoveries show us more and more the wonders of the heavens - they are magnificent! So is the rest of creation—man himself being the greatest creation of all. Each wonder teaches us about our Creator, His power and His plan. As we learn more about His creation, we come to know the Creator in a more intimate way than ever before. His wonders in the heavens make us ask, *"What is man that You are mindful of him?"*

REMEMBER: As we gaze in wonder at the stars of heaven, let us remember that our hearts are made to worship the God who created them.

STUDY

A teenager being raised in a Christian home asked, "Why did God make it so hard to discover His truth?" The godly mother replied, "It is like a diamond buried in the earth—the harder it is to find and polish, the more dear it is." So it is true that we must study and spend our time and energy on learning the things of God—and they are worth it!

Christians are called "disciples" - another word for students, and as Christ's disciples we are required to *"take up our cross daily and follow [Him]"*. In the school of discipleship, we are not given a desk and books, we learn from *"the things we suffer"*. Hebrews tells us that even Christ Jesus learned obedience by the things He suffered. There is no easier way for us. You see, we are not learning letters and numbers in the school of discipleship to which Christ calls us. We are learning to bend our wills to the will of our Heavenly Father.

We are also to learn holiness for we are to be like Christ. Accepting God's love means that we let Him work within us to produce His love in our hearts and *"grow up into the image of Christ"* as the Apostle Paul put it. Of course, His image in us only becomes perfect when we see Him. Paul also said, *"When we see Him, we shall be like Him, for we shall see Him as he is. For now we see in a glass darkly, but then face to face."*

Beyond this, we are to study God's Word so that we can understand it "rightly" in order to know how to live in holiness, obedience and love for it is in God's Word that we find **the truth of God, the plan of God and the power of God.** We can't live the Christian life without Christ!

REMEMBER: We are commanded to "study to show yourself approved unto God", and "Study to be quiet." These goals require effort - we only get them by studying!

TALK

"A man of words and not of deeds is like a garden full of weeds." So goes the old saying. People have always recognized that talk by itself is worthless. James wrote of those who tell their suffering neighbors to "be warmed and filled" without giving them heat or food. He said such talk is useless. He said that if we say we have faith, but don't act like it, we are "dead".

Still, we are not to devaluate loving words, given from a caring heart and accompanied by actions which underline their truth. Our speech reveals what is in our hearts just like an accent tells the trained ear the homeland of a traveler. Paul wrote that we are to be *"sound in speech which is beyond reproach, in order that the opponent may be put to shame, having nothing bad to say about us"* (Titus 2:8). Our words are to clearly announce that our hearts belong to God who loves us all and cares about each one.

We are to be caring people whose words communicate the love in our hearts. Paul wrote, *"Let your speech always be with grace, seasoned, as it were, with salt, so that you may know how you should respond to each person"* (Col. 4:6). How can an unheeding world know about a loving God? They can hear it in what we say ... and the way we say it.

James wrote that our words are like the small rudder of a very large ship - they can direct the entire weight of our lives even though words are only one part of life. We can sail the ship of our lives into troubled waters (or into a safe haven) by our words. He goes on to say that words are like a small fire - they cannot be extinguished and given opportunity, they can spread rapidly and do a great deal of damage as fire can do in a forest (James 3:3-5).

REMEMBER: We have two ears and only one mouth so that we can listen twice as much as we talk.

TEMPT

It is important to remember that although we are tempted to sin, it is not a sin to be tempted. The sin only occurs if and when we give in to the temptations that come our way. God has promised that we will not be tempted beyond our ability to trust Him to keep us from the temptation, so when we give in to temptation, it is because we have decided to follow that path - God's grace is sufficient to keep us from it if we call upon Him. James says that there is a *"crown of life"* (James 1:12) laid up for those who resist the power of temptation. Every temptation we face is a common experience for us all.

The story is told of a boy named Mark who wasn't very good at spelling. During a test, he succumbed to the temptation to copy from his neighbor's paper in order to get a passing grade. He successfully copied several words, but his teacher noticed what he was doing. She said nothing. At the end of the test, she saw that Mark was struggling with himself over his cheating. Finally, Mark tore up his paper. He decided not to accept a grade which he had not earned. The teacher called him to her side and commended his decision. She said, "Mark, today you have passed a much greater examination than your spelling test."

How true! A decision to maintain honesty is more important than how well you spell. It is also possible to go back and learn to spell correctly, but once we yield to temptation, it gets harder to make the right decision. Just so, each right choice helps us when next we are tempted. Just as the teacher encouraged Mark in doing right, so Christ helps us to make good decisions by His power even when we are not strong enough by ourselves.

REMEMBER: When you are trying to master temptation, let Christ master you and you will find that He makes a way out for you.

THINK

Thinking is the mind at work - creating an idea, forming an opinion, working toward understanding someone or something. The importance of our thoughts cannot be underestimated for Solomon wrote, *"As a man thinketh ... so is he"* (Prov. 23:7). Jesus said, *"Not what goes into the mouth defiles a man; but what comes out of the mouth, this defiles a man"* (Matt. 15:11). Jesus went on to say, *"Those things which proceed out of the mouth come from the heart, and they defile a man"* (Matt. 15:19). The thoughts we think originate in our hearts and if our hearts are evil, we think evil thoughts and speak evil with our mouths.

In the same way, the words of a good man or woman reflect the innermost thoughts of their hearts for a good tree does not bear bitter fruit. Christ said, *"O generation of vipers, how can you, being evil, speak good things?"* (Matt. 12:34). Solomon wrote, *"Keep thy heart with all diligence, for out of it are the issues of life"* (Prov. 4:23). The Bible also teaches us that what we do is controlled by what we think - our actions are the result of what we really think. Then, may I ask how important is our thought life? It's crucial! We must learn to control our thoughts, if we are going to turn our lives to that which is good.

Paul commanded us, *"Whatsoever things are true, whatsoever things are honest, whatsoever things are just, whatsoever things are pure and are lovely, whatsoever things are of good report ... THINK ON THESE THINGS"* (Phil. 4:8). We are not given any options here except to bend our minds to dwell on good things, then our hearts and our lives will also be filled with good things.

REMEMBER: "Thou wilt keep him in perfect peace whose mind is [filled] with [thoughts of] Thee, O God" (Isa. 26:3).

TIME

The history of development of instruments to measure time is very interesting. The Chaldeans who lived before the days of Abraham had set up a system of days and seasons based on a seven-day week. Even so, there didn't seem to be a way to reckon long periods of time and history was marked by outstanding events such as the Exodus or Passover, the Babylonian captivity or an earthquake as fixed points to indicate the timing of other events.

Although Scripture does not state specifically that time began at the Creation, it does clearly state that the day will come when *"time shall be no more"*. In eternity, there is no beginning, nor any ending, but for our planet and our universe, there was a definite beginning - and there will come an end. When viewed in this context, it is no wonder that our life is compared to *"a vapor which appears for a moment and vanishes away"* (Job 4:14).

Paul concurred for he said, *"Time is short ... this world passes away"* (I Cor. 7:29). Again he said, *"Walk in wisdom toward them that are without, redeeming the time"* (Col. 4:5). Clearly, we must do whatever good we are going to do NOW while we have time. The life we have been given is a treasure which we are to invest for God just as the servants were to do whose master had given them "talents" to invest. Some invested more wisely than others, but the only words of rebuke the master had were for the servant who failed to use his time and talent at all. Just so, we can please our Heavenly Father by using our lives to make the world a better place. Let us invest our time to accomplish the greatest good within our power.

REMEMBER: "Only one life, it will soon be past. Only what's done for Christ will last."

TITHE

The word itself means "a tenth". This ancient custom has never been changed in God's economy. We are still taught to give one-tenth of all we earn to God and His work. It is a SCRIPTURAL PRINCIPLE, not a human device put in place by some church or para-church organization. Moses taught *"The tenth shall be holy unto the Lord"* (Lev. 27:32). Jesus agreed, *"These ye ought to have done"* (Matt. 23:23).

Tithing is given as a BIBLICAL MINIMUM. This is not given as the total of what we can give. It is given as the least we can do, with gifts and offerings to be given over and above that which is required. Tithing is also a CHRISTIAN WITNESS. Our faith is an unseen quality, but our actions, the habits of our lives such as tithing, are plain indicators of the faith in our hearts. Also, tithing is an ACKNOWLEDGMENT OF OWNERSHIP for we belong to God and all that we have, all that we possess is His. What we earn and own is given to us in trust by a loving heavenly Father and by giving Him the first tithe of all, we say that we know it really belongs to Him - we are His stewards.

Tithing is a TOKEN OF CONSECRATION, speaking to all of our devotion to God - not in words only, but also in our possessions. It is also a TOKEN OF DEVOTION for we do not give from duty, but from hearts overflowing with the goodness of God (II Chron. 31:5). Our tithes are an EXPRESSION OF GRATITUDE for God has supported and sustained us with food, shelter and all the other things we need for life on this planet. Moreover, tithing is an ADVENTURE IN BLESSING because God has promised to flood us with blessings if we will tithe.

REMEMBER: Not only do "we love Him because He first loved us," we also give to Him because He has first given to us.

TOGETHER

The current word for "togetherness" is "synergism" and it highlights the fact that when people or forces come together, they can accomplish more than any one of them could accomplish alone. One writer put it this way:

"In the Old Testament the idea is captured by the phrase, *'It is not good that man should dwell alone'*. Jesus went further to say, *'Where two or three are gathered together in My name, there am I in the midst.'* Both point to our essential nature as social beings designed for one another, and when related properly with Christ at the center, we become a synergism, greater together than the sum of our individualism.

"Biblical synergism finds its roots in the doctrine of the Trinity. God is plurality within unity, three Persons living in perfect oneness as Father, Son and Holy Spirit, thus producing an effect greater than the sum of the individual parts. Because God is three, He can relate to man as transcendent, cosmic Judge, yet also as Redeemer and Friend. In the New Testament, synergism blooms fully in the pattern of Jesus with His disciples. Jesus called His disciples to live and serve in the context of a loving, supportive community. When He sent them out to evangelize, it was two by two. Together they became the apostolic band a synergism, a body greater than the sum of the parts.

"Although Paul was one of history's great personalities, he never chose to work alone. At Antioch, Paul worked along with Barnabas and a team of elders and teachers. On his missionary journeys, he traveled with Barnabas, John Mark, Silas, Timothy and Luke."

REMEMBER: Sanctified synergism multiplies God's grace, brings blessing on earth and glory to the name of our Heavenly Father.

TREASURY

This word refers to a storehouse set aside for valuable things only. Jesus was interested in what people held in value so He situated Himself across from the treasury in the Temple and watched the people place their offerings into it. As He watched, the wealthy came and deposited large amounts of money - their treasures. Still, Jesus was not impressed for they gave out of their abundance and it cost them no sacrifice whatsoever.

As he watched, however, a poor widow came and placed her tiny gift into the treasury box with no fanfare or pride in her gift at all. She quietly gave her gift to God and went on her way—humbly, meekly. Jesus saw giving in terms of what people had left, however, not in terms of what they had given. From this point of view, the gift of the widow was the greatest for she had nothing left at all! She had given her last pennies to her Heavenly Father. She had not calculated how much she would need for food or rent - she did not have enough for either. Still, rather than try to satisfy her most basic needs, she saw it as more necessary to give something to God - and she did just that!

How do you decide how much to give to the Lord and His work? Do you make sure FIRST that your bills are all paid and there is enough left to do some of the things you want to do? If you give God what's left after that, I'm sure that your gifts are small. Even if you give large sums, the gifts are small for you have considered yourself first instead of giving to God first, then managing on what you have left for yourself.

I'm sure that God supplied for that widow! She may not have eaten steak, but she was satisfied with the food that God gave her - of that I'm sure!

REMEMBER: Giving sacrificially is a grace - failing to give is a disgrace!

TREE

So ancient is this word that we find it in the account of Creation given in Genesis one. *"God made grow every tree that is pleasant to the sight, and good for food"* (Gen. 2:9). It is there that we read of the Tree of Life for God placed a flaming sword to keep Adam and Eve from it after they had sinned. This same Tree of Life is spoken of in Revelation and its *"leaves were for the healing of the nations"*.

Trees figure prominently in Scripture in many ways. Adam and Eve hid among the trees when they had sinned and feared to face God. We use trees today to help supply our food and to provide materials for our homes and buildings as well as the many other uses we have devised. A tree was used to make a cradle for the Savior no doubt since Joseph was a carpenter. Then, the Roman soldiers made a rugged cross for Jesus when they put Him to death. Zacchaeus climbed a tree to see Jesus. The cedars of Lebanon were used in the construction of the Temple in Jerusalem. Olive trees produced oil for Jesus and made a haven for Him when He knelt to pray.

Psalm one describes a tree, planted by a river—perenially green and producing fruit in season. Such a tree "prospers", we are told. The comparison to such a tree is linked to the person who turns away from the ungodly and gives himself to the study of God's Word, delighting in it and finding strength and health. Trees stand in one place and offer to everyone who passes, the fruit they produce, the shade and relief they can give, and the slient testimony to a Heavenly Father who supplies all the needs of so great a living thing as a tree.

REMEMBER: We are more valuable than God's trees. If He cares for them, supplying all their needs, surely He will care for us as well.

TRIBULATION

There is a strange philosophy which seems to pervade the thinking of almost everyone, including Christians. We all tend to think that if we only had a little more money, or better health, or a happier family life, or ... something, we would "have it made". We don't seem to grasp that Scripture tells us repeatedly that *"In the world, we will have tribulation"*. *"Man is born to trouble as the sparks fly upward,"* the Proverbs tell us - and it's true! It is futile to fix our attention on something - anything - and expect that life will be a bed of roses, if only we can achieve it.

A lot of our tribulations are just the ordinary hassles of life - whatever life hands us–those things over which we have no control, yet have to cope with every day. It may be a fatherless child, a crippled body, a homely face, an outstandingly beautiful face, an ethnic identity, or any one of a thousand other things. We are born into circumstances about which we have no choice.

Other times, tribulation comes to us as a result of our actions and/or our decisions. Too often, we displease the Lord and He sends tribulation into our lives to call us back to Himself. Other times, He is teaching and training us by means of the tribulations of our lives. *"Tribulation works patience,"* we read and in time we come to see that God uses the difficulties of life to build good things into us. Tribulation is not a curse—it's a blessing! God loves us enough to measure out for us just the exact amount of trouble we need to learn what He wants us to know. He only uses the tribulations of life to bring about His will in our lives. The question is asked in Scripture, *"Shall we accept good from the hand of God and not trouble?"* The answer is clear - we are to be willing to accept both from our Heavenly Father.

REMEMBER: "All things work together for good" in God's plans for us.

TROUBLE

Often when we use the word "trouble" we are referring to distress of some kind - "troubled waters", "a troubled spirit", "trouble on every side". Often, we are really talking about our reaction to tribulation more than the difficulty itself. We are tossed around, pushed into a corner by trials and we feel distressed - "troubled". We can't do very much about some of the difficulties of life. We just have to live with a lot of things.

Still, Jesus said, *"Let not your heart be troubled,"* and we wonder how we can keep from being distressed by the injustices and unfairness that greet us on every side in this life. However, Jesus did not just give us a commandment, He also told us how to keep it. He said, *"You believe in God, believe also in Me."* When we are trusting God to lead and guide us, knowing that all things are under His control, we actually CAN live through trouble without being troubled by it.

We are also assigned a guardian angel to deliver us from trouble when we call upon God. *"This poor man cried and the Lord heard him, And saved him out of all his troubles. The angel of the Lord encamps around those who fear Him and delivers them (from their troubles)"* (Ps. 34:6-7). God Himself has invited us to call upon Him when we're in trouble. He urges us to come to Him with our problems and He has promised to hear us. One of America's founding fathers wrote, "Shall we not accept medicine from the hand of the physician? If it is bitter, we know he gives it for our ultimate good and can endure the distress for the benefit it is designed to accomplish."

REMEMBER: We don't need to look for trouble, but when it comes, look to the Lord - He will give strength for the day and deliverance!

UNBELIEF

The Governor of Florida was my host in his office in Tallahassee. I asked what his favorite Bible verse was and he replied, "I don't know where it is found, but the verse says, *'Lord, I believe; help thou my unbelief'*" (Mark 9:24).

Unbelief is not the same as disbelief which indicates an active rejection of the proposition at hand. Unbelief can merely indicate a lack of believing - a neglect of considering and acting upon that which is taught. It is amazing to find people who have seen and heard enough to believe in something who go on living their lives as though they never heard. Believing indicates that things are different because of the convictions we hold.

For instance, Jesus said that "*all things are possible to him that believes*" and yet we find ourselves limited on every side. The Roman soldier to whom Jesus said those words, however, tried to believe and he cried out, "*Lord, I believe; help thou my unbelief.*" Like that man, we are frequently aware of the limits of our faith and, therefore, the limits of God's power in our lives. Remember, though, that God urges us to come "boldly" to Him and to ask for the things we long for in our lives.

Dwight L. Moody's life goal was to see what God could do in his life, yet when he died, Mr. Moody said, "The world has YET to see what God can do in one man's life." None of us reach the outer limits of God's power in our lives. We do not face the challenges of life alone, but at every turn, and in every circumstance, we can look to our Heavenly Father to supply that which we do not possess and enable us to do that which is beyond our strength. He is able!

REMEMBER: Go forward as far as you can by faith. Then, reject unbelief and look to God to lead you on.

UNDERSTAND

Not many of us are able to see things for what they really are. Reality is hard to accept sometimes and we prefer to ignore and set aside some of the things that might trouble us the most. It seems that we can hardly **"stand"** to understand sometimes. The other half of the word, **"under,"** indicates the depth of understanding - it is not a surface thing. Understanding is more than knowledge - it is the grasping of what knowledge implies.

Solomon, the wisest man who ever lived, wrote first and at length about wisdom and understanding. He teaches us that loving God is *"the beginning of wisdom"* and he goes on to say that *"they that seek the Lord understand all things"* (Prov. 28:5). Hebrews put it this way, *"By faith, **we understand** ...."*

It is our understanding that God is in control of what appears to be an "out of control" world that brings us peace and enables us to accept those things in life which are painful. In "thinking God's thoughts after Him", we find a reason and a purpose for life and all its trials. When we see things from God's perspective, we gain some understanding of what it is He is doing in this world - and in our lives. When we know Him, we understand what's happening to us and to the world. Why would God prolong the sufferings of the world? His heart breaks at the pain and oppression He sees among us. Why then, why doesn't He bring it to and end and set things straight? Peter wrote that God is *"longsuffering toward us, not willing that any should perish but that all should come to repentance"* (II Peter 3:9). So we see that God is at work, extending His mercy and salvation as long as there are those who will come to Him and find peace for their souls. Doesn't He care? He cares very much and He has a plan.

REMEMBER: *"They that seek the Lord understand all things"* - there is no limit to what we can receive from God.

UNSPOTTED

At our house, we have some tablecloths that, even when washed clean, still bear some spots. When an article has been used, but cleaned up to the point that it has no spots, we say it is "like new" - unspotted. The description here is one of perfection and purity.

One of the tragedies of our day is the accidental oil spills that spoil the coastline for miles when they occur, and birds, whose life can be threatened by even a drop of oil, are covered with the thick goo that floats on top of the water. It is amazing how little it takes to ruin some things. Even our parents and grandparents said, "One rotten apple spoils the whole." Just like the drop of oil or the bad apple, so Christians can have their testimonies taken from them by what may seem to be a small matter. "A good name is rather to be chosen than great riches," we read in Proverbs and once lost, it is not easy to re-establish it.

Noah sent two birds from the ark - a raven and a dove. The raven did not return to the ark even though the waters had not yet receded from the earth. It could scavenge food from the floating debris and did not seek to make a home for itself. The dove, on the other hand, returned to Noah when she found no tree in which to make a home for herself. Not being a scavenger, she sought new growth on which to feed and found none. Only after the waters receded did she remain outside of the ark and begin her life again. That is our choice, too. We can scavenge off whatever rotting debris we may find, or we can wait to find a life that is clean and new - free from the contamination of the world. "Is your life a shining witness with a testimony true? Could the world be won to Jesus just by what they see in you?" (Adams).

REMEMBER: The Christian must live in the world, but he should not let the world live in him.

UPHARSIN

This is one of the words that the armless hand wrote on the wall of Belshazzar's banquet hall. God told him that he had been "weighed in the balances and found wanting" and that his kingdom would be divided and given to the Medes and the Persians. Upharsin means, *"Your kingdom is divided"*. For Belshazzar and his generals, it meant death at the hands of their enemies.

Billy Graham tells of a young man who was dying. When roused, he said, "Leave me alone. Can't you see I'm busy dying?" This seems to be what so many around us say when we try to awaken them to spiritual things. They are dying and don't want to be distracted. It is their souls that perish without God.

We, too, have been warned of our failure to measure up - we are found "wanting" just as Belshazzar was. *"The wages of sin is death,"* we are told in Romans 6:23. Impending doom awaits us unless we have found *"eternal life through Jesus Christ our Lord"*. Our judgment is just as sure, our destruction just as complete as that which befell the ancient Babylonians in that vast banquet hall when their enemies poured in before they knew they were coming. God must punish sin for He is righteous and cannot bear its presence.

He has provided for us, however, by making salvation available to us through Jesus Christ. We are not doomed to death and judgment! We can have life in Christ Jesus our Lord. Today is the day of salvation. Today, if we hear His voice, let us call upon Him for the gift of salvation which He has provided. Claim Jesus' blood as payment for your sins and ask Him to wash you whiter than snow while there is still time.

REMEMBER: "Believe in your heart that God has raised him (Jesus) from the dead [and] you will be saved" (Rom.10:9).

UPHOLD

This may be the most comforting word in the Bible for every time it is used, God is reminding His children that He will care for them. *"The arms of the wicked shall be broken, but the Lord upholds the righteous"* (Ps. 37:17). *"The Lord upholds all that fall, and raises up all those who are bowed down"* (Ps. 145:14). After David had sinned, he prayed, *"Restore to me the joy of Thy salvation, and uphold me with a willing spirit"* (Ps. 51:12). David prayed, *"Uphold me according to Thy word, that I may live; and let me not be ashamed of my hope"* (Ps. 119:116).

A minister shared a train compartment with a discouraged young man who felt that he could bear life no longer. The minister took a knife from his pocket and declared that he would make it stand on end on the cover of his Bible in spite of the rocking train. The young man was skeptical and said so! The minister looked at the knife in his hand and said, "I'm already doing it!" The young man laughed. "But you are holding it - that's how it can stand." "Did you ever hear of one standing on end without being held up?" inquired the minister. The young man saw clearly that (like the knife) he could not stand without the strong hand of God to hold him.

David learned to use the strength that God gives when he was a young man guarding his father's sheep, so when he faced Goliath, he knew that he could call on God for more strength than he alone possessed. He said to Goliath, "You come to me with a sword and with a spear and with a shield: but I come to you in the name of the Lord of Hosts, the God of Israel, whom you have defied." David was protected by God's angels–he was safe.

REMEMBER: Creation of the heavens was "fingerwork" to God. Salvation was accomplished with His right arm, and He upholds us with His loving hand.

VESSEL

This word may refer to anything from a small vase to an oceangoing ship and can be made of valuable materials such as gold and silver or a more common substance such as clay used to make a ceramic pot. God speaks of people as being vessels and acknowledges that (like material vessels) people vary in value and in use from the the very dear to the very common.

Have you ever gone to the dishwasher to find a clean dish only to discover that no one had bothered to turn on the helpful machine and the "vessels" were still dirty? Just so, God's vessels must be washed - cleansed from sin and ready for use in the hand of God. *"If anyone cleanses himself, he will be a vessel for honor, sanctified and useful for the Master, prepared for every good work"* (II Tim. 2:21). We are ready to be useful when we are washed in the blood of the Lamb of God, cleansed from sin and made fit to serve our Savior.

None of us begins as a clean vessel and none of us can keep clean without coming to God. *"If we confess our sins, He is faithful and just to forgive us our sins and to cleanse us from all unrighteousness"* (I Jn. 1:9). Most of all, we are not to make the claim that we have not sinned for God's word clearly tells us that **all of us** have sinned and need the marvelous cleansing of God in our lives. Once sanctified by Jesus' blood, we are to live in such a way as to bring honor to our Savior. When we need to be washed again, we come to Him for the daily refreshing and cleansing that we need. The purity of our God requires that we also keep our lives pure. He has said that we are to be *"holy as He is holy"*. We can only be holy as He cleanses us.

REMEMBER: God's standard of holiness is perfect. We never achieve perfection here on earth, but we are constantly to seek His cleansing.

VICTORY

Although we usually associate victory with rejoicing, this is not always the case. When Absalom led a rebellion against his father, King David, he was defeated, but David's victory was turned to mourning for Absalom died and the King grieved for his son (II Sam. 19:2). David's general, Joab, felt that it was improper for David to grieve for so treacherous a son and that he should rejoice with those who had loyally served the King. David knew well that victory belongs to God. He said, *"Thine, O Lord, is the greatness, and the power, and the glory, and the victory and the majesty"* (I Chron. 29:13).

Death seems to be the greatest enemy of man for every life ends in death, and yet, Paul wrote, *"Death is swallowed up in victory. O death, where is thy sting? O grave, where is thy victory?"* (I Cor. 15:54-55). How could he make this brave statement? He knew that the resurrection of Jesus Christ teaches us that death is NOT THE END of all for us, but we will be raised from the dead as Christ was raised - never to be subject to death again.

"We shall all be changed. In a moment, in the twinkling of an eye, at the last trump; for the trumpet shall sound, and the dead shall be raised incorruptible, and we shall be changed. For this corruptible must put on incorruption, and this mortal must put on immortality. Thanks be to God, who gives us the victory through our Lord Jesus Christ" (I Cor. 15:51-53, 57).

No, death is not the end - it is only one battle and the ultimate victory lies in our faith in God and in His Son, Jesus Christ who died and rose again to give us victory over death.

REMEMBER: "Whatsoever is born of God overcomes the world: and this is the victory that overcomes the world, even our faith" (I Jn. 5:4).

VISIT

One Bible commentator writes, "It was no mere social call that would have met the need of the prisoner. Oriental prisons were cold and uncomfortable. A prisoner needed ministering care. Jesus taught that to visit those in jail in this sympathetic and sacrificial way was like ministering directly to Him." We see that in the Bible, to visit has deeper significance than the word as we use it today.

When John the Baptist was born according to the promise of God, his father Zacharias said, *"Blessed be the Lord God of Israel; for He has visited and redeemed His people. The dayspring from on high has visited us."* (Lk. 1:68). He was speaking not of John the Baptist, but of Jesus Christ the promised Redeemer of Israel. His visit to this earth was for the purpose of ministering to the people of the world–He **"visited"** His people.

This is corroborated in Jesus' statement as He wept over Jerusalem and said, *"You did not know the day of thy visitation"* (Lk. 19:44). Jesus had come from heaven to earth - and the Jews would not accept Him! Many looked to Him for release from Roman oppression, but most of them did not recognize the Messiah whom God had sent to release them from the power of sin. To those who accepted Him as God's Son, however, He gave salvation even to the thief on the Cross in his last hour.

As believers, we are not only to visit others, ministering to them in the name of Jesus, we are also to invite them into our homes *"without grudging"* (I Peter 4:9). James wrote that our faith can be measured by our willingness to *"visit the fatherless and the widows"*.

REMEMBER: It takes more than talk to demonstrate our faith to a doubting world. Our deeds must match our words.

VOICE

Each person's voice is as distinctive as his fingerprints. Speech patterns and quality of sound vary with each individual and none is the same as any other. God's voice, too, is uniquely His own. When Adam and Eve heard God's voice in the Garden of Eden after they had disobeyed Him, they hid themselves, knowing that they had sinned.

When Cain had killed Abel and God asked him what he had done, God said, *"The voice of thy brother's blood cries unto me from the ground"* (Gen. 4:9-10). This time, "voice" was used in a figurative sense, but usually, the Bible refers to an audible voice when this word is used. God **spoke** to Noah, telling him to build an ark. God **called** Abraham to leave Ur of the Chaldees and go to a land which He would show him. God **commissioned** Moses to lead the Israelites out of Egypt.

When God's people sinned, however, God refused to speak to them until they repented. They asked for a man to be appointed to tell them what God wanted them to hear, so God gave them judges who spoke on God's behalf. Later, God gave them prophets who used the phrase, *"Thus saith the Lord...."*

Many verses refer to God's voice in water, thunder, power, majesty, flame, shaking of the wilderness, and in many other ways. Elijah heard God in a *"still, small voice"* (I Kings 19), but ultimately, God spoke to us all *"by His Son"* (Heb. 1:1-2). God gave His Son to say to us, "I love you" (Jn. 3:16). Jesus came to do His Father's will ... and speak His Father's words, if you will. In turn, the Father's voice was heard from heaven saying, *"This is My beloved Son: hear Him"* (Mk. 9:7).

REMEMBER: Just as the eyes are the window of the soul, so our voices reveal what is in our hearts. Oh Lord, set a seal upon our lips!

VOID

This old-fashioned word is found very near the beginning of God's Word when it says, *"The earth was without form and void"* (Gen. 1:2). The shapeless mass of our planet was empty - nothing lived here at that point in time - no plants, no animals, no fish, no birds, no people. Void doesn't mean sparse - it means empty! God's voice was used to create the sun, moon, and stars as well as the plant and animal worlds. God's crown of creation, mankind, is great because we are created in God's image (nothing else is) because God gave us *"a living soul"*.

In Numbers 30, we find this word used concerning the vows a woman made either while in her father's house or in her husband's house. In giving men the leadership of the home, God gave them the authority to "void" (make empty) the vows of their daughters or wives under certain conditions. They must do it immediately, and if they make them void "in any manner" later, the men must bear the punishment for the broken vow. This Old Testament law placed awesome responsibility on men of that day.

God's Word can be made "void", too, by rebellious people who will not hear nor heed what God has said. In Psalm 119:126, the writer calls upon God to punish those who treat His words so carelessly. Proverbs uses the word to indicate that some people are completely lacking in wisdom or understanding. Paul wrote that he wanted to be *"void of offense toward God and man"* (Acts 24:16). Mostly, though, Paul sought to make his life count and resisted anything which might cause his witness to become "void" or ineffective toward the saving of men's souls. Paul bent every effort to preach the Gospel of Jesus Christ and to convince men of sin, of righteousness and of judgment.

REMEMBER: Tell everyone you meet what God has said because He said, "It shall not return unto Me void."

WILL

As with so many simple things, the word "will" has many uses and requires a lot of other words to explain just what it means. We refer to our determination as our "will", and although we all know what is meant by it, we are hardpressed to explain how we come to have the will to do something or to refrain from doing it. Our last wishes are designated as our "will" and how we feel toward others is called "good will" or "ill will".

The Bible uses this little word about 4,000 times - it is very important. Serious-minded Christians are interested in God's will and seek to please Him in all that they do. A.W. Tozer stated that "peace of heart depends on knowing that God is actually guiding, and their failure to be sure that He is, destroys inward tranquility and fills them with uncertainty and fear. It is absolutely essential that we be completely dedicated to God's high honor and be surrendered to the Lordship of Jesus Christ. God will not lead us except for His own glory and He cannot lead us if we resist His will. Instead of trying to employ God to achieve our ends, we must submit ourselves joyously to God and let Him work through us to achieve His own ends."

God's will includes four things - those things about which He has said an emphatic **"No"**; those things about which He has said an emphatic **"Yes"**; those things about which we are to decide based on our own **sanctified preferences**; and those rare matters which require some **special guidance** from God. God is not like a lenient parent who will give in to the desires of a petulant child. God will not contradict Himself. His "No" means no. His "Yes" means yes. Above all, He has promised to guide us.

REMEMBER: It is useless to try to persuade God in contradiction to His Word. He loves us so much, He will not spoil us by insincerity.

WORD

In the world of communication, a single word is the smallest unit by which a thought can be expressed. Many among us have some understanding of how important a single word can be when used correctly ... or incorrectly. One Sunday School teacher began to examine the words of the Scripture assignment for each week. He went to the Greek to find the original word used. Then he sought words that meant the same thing, or something similar. Each one cast a ray of light on a different aspect of the others.

Proverbs 25:11 tells us that *"A word fitly spoken is like apples of gold in pictures of silver"*. How welcome is the person who can offer the word that is needed in a time of stress ... or distress. How abrasive the person who babbles on meaninglessly in a time of suffering or loss. God's Word teaches us that we are to be very careful about what we say - for we will "give account" of each word when we stand before God.

Jesus is called ***"The Word"*** for He was the expression of the Godhead to mankind and His life tells us all that we need to know about God. His coming to earth from heaven clearly conveys to us that we are loved! The power He exercised in healing everyone that came to Him and raising the dead speaks volumes about the almighty ability of God to accomplish whatever He wishes to do. The tenderness of Jesus as small children were drawn to His side and He would not let them be moved aside, tells us that God is not so interested in greatness as in the open heart of those who come to Him. His attention to every request helps us to know that God will hear us when we come to Him in prayer concerning the intimate matters of our lives.

REMEMBER: "In the beginning was the Word and the Word was with God and the Word WAS GOD" (Jn. 1:1). Jesus is God ... in a word!

WRONG

We don't like to be wrong, do we? We've all seen someone (or have been that someone) who tried to explain away wrong and make it seem right. If we're wrong because we didn't **know** any better, we appear foolish. If we're wrong because we didn't **do** any better, we appear guilty. Either way, it is an uncomfortable situation and we often do strange things to extricate ourselves from it.

We will be held accountable for those things we do that are wrong. When we are wronged, we can trust in our God to see that it is made right in His time. There is a great deal that is wrong with the world we live in ... so much so that some among us say that there is no distinction between right and wrong. How can we tell? Isn't one person's idea of right just as good as another's? Isn't it all relative? No, the Bible makes it clear that God is the One who sets the standard for right and wrong.

"The ways of the Lord are right, and the just shall walk in them; but the transgressors shall fall in them" (Hosea 14:9).

The only thing relative about **right** is whether or not we do things God's way! God has the last word and in it, He will "make or break us" according to what He says is right and wrong.

"Whatsoever you do, do it heartily, as to the Lord, and not unto men: knowing that of the Lord you shall receive the reward of the inheritance: for you serve the Lord Christ. But he that does wrong shall receive for the wrong which he has done: and there is no respect of persons" (Col. 3:23-25). God will punish wrong - no matter whose wrong it is!

REMEMBER: No matter who you are - high and mighty or lowly - you never have the right to do that which is wrong in God's sight.

YESTERDAY

Although this word is found several places in the Bible, there is one Old Testament and one New Testament reference that stand out. The first says, *"From everlasting to everlasting, Thou art God ... for a thousand years in Thy sight are but yesterday when it is past, and as a watch in the night"* (Ps. 90). The idea here is to underline the vast difference between God and mankind for to us, a thousand years is a long time, but to God it is like a three-hour "watch in the night". We can compare a minute and a million years, but we cannot make a comparison between "time and eternity [for] there is none," said Matthew Henry.

When yesterday is gone, it cannot be recovered. We glibly say, "You can't change history," but the truth of that statement is tremendous! It holds powerful meaning for our lives.

In the New Testament, we read, *"Jesus Christ, the same yesterday, today and forever"* (Heb. 13:8). Not only do we learn from this that we can count on Jesus to remain unchanged in a changing world, we can also conclude that what we know of Him will always be true.

Have you ever returned to a scenic place of your childhood and found the trees, the rocks, the hills to be the same? It is reassuring to know that though your life may have taken many turns, there are those things which have remained as they were. How much more important to remember that Jesus, the One who loves us and cares for us, has not changed, but loves and cares for us still. Jesus, whose power was displayed at the creation of the world, is powerful still. Jesus, who spared nothing to save our souls, still uses His life on our behalf.

REMEMBER: Jesus was God before He came to earth. In earthly form, He was still God. When He returns for us, He will come as Almighty God!

YIELD

We think of yielding as "giving in", but it also means "giving forth" for the trees yield their fruit and the fields of the farmer yield their crops. When a soul comes to the end of life on earth, the body yields the spirit - lets it go from its earthly home to its eternal destination.

Each of these various meanings has spiritual significance for we *"yield ourselves as instruments of righteousness"* by giving in to the work of the Holy Spirit in our lives. As believers we also bear the fruit of the Spirit - our lives giving forth *"love, joy, peace, longsuffering, gentleness, goodness"* and all the other evidences of His presence in our lives.

In everyday life, however, we often think of yielding in terms of being coerced into complying with a superior force and this is not the case in spiritual things. God does not twist our arm behind our back until we say, "Uncle!" He calls upon us to give ourselves over to Him, but He waits to see what we will do. He pictures for us the joys of bearing the fruit of the Spirit, but He only makes it possible. He does not force us to become fruitbearers nor does He require that we join Him in heaven, for we can refuse His invitation, if we will.

Jesus said, *"I stand at the door and knock. IF any man hear my voice, and open the door, I will come in to him and sup with him and he with Me"* (Rev. 3:10). Jesus knocks, but He does not force the door of your heart open so that He can come in. Jesus is knocking today and waiting to see if you will yield your will to Him. Won't you let Him in today? What joys are waiting for those of us who let Him in! Jesus' presence, His supply, His great goodness all come in when He enters.

REMEMBER: You and I can yield ourselves to Jesus Christ and allow Him to have full control of our lives.

YOU

Have you ever read a letter that was not addressed to you? When doing so, you had to replace every "you" with the name of the person to whom the letter was addressed. Some people read the Bible that way - as if it were written to someone else, but Peter said, *"The promise is to YOU!"* (Acts 2:39). This points out clearly that Christianity is for each one of us. Salvation, forgiveness, redemption and heaven are offered to every one of us individually. That's a marvelous assurance!

When someone wins the ten million dollar sweepstakes, that's nice, but if YOU were to win it, it would revolutionize your life. So, don't just hear the words, *"Jesus Christ died to save sinners"*, hear that He died to save YOU! That's more precious than the sweepstakes prize. That makes it possible for you to say, "Jesus is MY Savior, MY Friend, MY Redeemer and MY King!"

Johannes von Mueller was a Swiss historian and as he studied ancient times, he always felt that something was missing. When in the course of his life, he read the New Testament and placed Jesus Christ into the history which was his life's study, He found that history is actually HIS Story–the story of God's dealings with mankind through the giving of His Son, Jesus.

"God so loved the world that He gave His only begotten Son that whosoever believes in Him should not perish, but have everlasting life. For God sent not His Son into the world to condemn the world, but that the world through Him might have life" (Jn. 3:16-17). All of human history is the story of God speaking to the people of the world about sin, judgment and salvation. That's why Jesus came.

REMEMBER: "He that believes on Him is not condemned; but he that believes not is condemned already" (John 3:18).

YOUNG

Although this word can mean youthful and immature, we find that Scripture uses it at times to illustrate the contrasts of God's dealings with mankind. In the future reign of Christ, we read that *"the wolf shall dwell with the lamb, and the leopard shall lie down with the kid; and the calf and the young lion and the fatling together; and a little child (a young one) shall lead them"* (I Kings 11:6).

Jesus' early life illustrates this same idea for when He was a young child, the wisemen fell down and worshipped Him and He was still young when He stayed in the Temple discussing weighty issues with the Scribes and Pharisees there. His parents did not understand that Jesus had work to do for His Heavenly Father that was more important than any earthly work He might do.

There have always been differences between young and old, and I suppose there always will be. The older ones desire desperately to pass on to the younger the wisdom gained through years of working and worrying. The younger ones never can believe that the older generation really understands the world in which they are growing up, the things that are important to them.

How amazing then, to discover that Jesus can satisfy the hearts of young and old alike. Faith in God does not belong to the older generation, nor does the younger generation discover truths not formerly available to the older. We are all made in God's image and He knows how to meet the needs of young and old alike. He tells the young to *"Remember now thy Creator in the days of your youth"*, and He reminds the older ones that they still have *"a future and a hope"* for God has *"plans for you"*, too.

REMEMBER: It is not our age or understanding that impresses God, but the openness of our hearts to hear Him and follow the Shepherd of our souls.

ZION

Here is a name that is like music to the Jewish ear. It is the name of the most sacred hill of Jerusalem. Long centuries ago, it was the city where the Jebusites lived in David's childhood and he loved that place although the name meant "dowtrodden–a no-man's land". David captured the city and made it his capitol, renaming it Jerusalem, "dwelling place of peace".

At a United Nations conference, an Israeli proclaimed, "Whan the Jews, exiled from their land in the seventh century before the Christian era, sat by the rivers of Babylon and wept, but also prayed and sought ways to go home, that was already ZIONism. When in a mass revolt against their exile, they returned and rebuilt the Temple and re-established their State, that was ZIONism. When they were the last people in the Mediterranean basin to resist the forces of the Roman Empire and to struggle for independence, that was ZIONism. Uprooted by conquerors and dispersed by them all over the world, they continued to dream and to strive, and that was ZIONism. When Jews went to Hitler's gas chambers with the name of Jerusalem on their lips, that was ZIONism. ZIONism was not born in the Jewish ghettos of Europe, but on the battlefield against imperialism in ancient Israel. It is not an outmoded nationalistic revival but an unparalleled epic of centuries of resistance to force and bondange. Those who attack ZIONism attack the fundamental provisions of the United Nations Charter."

The Old Testament conveys how God formed Israel and has had a special plan for her. The Old Testament is Israel's history textbook and from Israel, God sent Jesus to be our Savior.

REMEMBER: "For Zion's sake ... I will not rest until her righteousness go forth as brightness, and her salvation as a lamp that burneth" (Isa.62:1).

Christian Projects Services, Inc.

La Habra CA 90631